Spitfire Mk. XVIe SL721 (C-GVZB) is one of the newest Spitfires to fly in Canada. It is currently owned by Michael Potter and is refinished in the markings of No. 421 Squadron RCAF and is now registered in Gatineau, Quebec as part of the Vintage Wings of Canada Collection.

SUPERMARINE
SPITFIRE

Dr Alfred Price

MIDLAND

An imprint of
Ian Allan Publishing

For Joshua

Acknowledgements

Among those supplying photographs which appear in this book were the Public Archives of Canada, Wojtek Matusiak and Peter Arnold.

Author's note

The correct German abbreviation for the Messerschmitt 109 and 110 was Bf 109 and Bf 110. However, during the war the Bf abbreviation was unknown in Britain and is therefore not to be found in any wartime official RAF report, the abbreviation Me 109 or Me 110 being used throughout. In the interests of authenticity, therefore, where a wartime RAF document is quoted verbatim in this book the Me abbreviation is retained.

Preface

I drew my first breath in August 1936, five months after the maiden flight of the Spitfire. Together we lived through the desperate times when Great Britain was beset by powerful foes, when, from the spring of 1940 to the autumn of 1942, British arms underwent an almost unbroken run of defeats. There was but one shining exception: the Battle of Britain in the summer of 1940. This pivotal action was fought out in the skies above southern England between the Spitfires and Hurricanes of RAF Fighter Command, and the Luftwaffe. Both RAF fighter types deserve credit in equal measure for securing that victory, yet there can be no denying that over the years the Spitfire has received the lion's share of public acclaim. It is not fair but history rarely is fair. Reginald Mitchell's shapely little fighter secured for itself a unique place in the British national psyche. Even today the sight and sound of a Spitfire passing overhead invokes deep feelings of nostalgia among those who lived through those dangerous times. And I am one of them.

Dr Alfred Price
Uppingham
Rutland

First published 2010

ISBN 978 1 85780 324 2

© Dr. Alfred Price
Project Editor and Production: Chevron Publishing Limited
© Colour profiles: Janusz Swiatlon and Tom Tullis
© Cover photograph: Philip Makanna 'GHOSTS' via Arthur Rayner. For more photographs visit www.ghosts.com
Chevron Publishing would like to thank Bruce Hales-Dutton, David Wadman, Tony Holmes and Arthur Rayner in the production of this publication.

Published by Midland Publishing
An imprint of Ian Allan Publishing Ltd, Riverside Business Park, Molesey Road, Hersham, Surrey, KT12 4RG
Printed by Ian Allan Printing Ltd, Riverside Business Park, Molesey Road, Hersham, Surrey, KT12 4RG
Distributed in the United States of America and Canada by BookMasters Distribution Services.

Visit the Ian Allan Publishing website at **www.ianallanpublishing.com**

CONTENTS

FOREWORD

Wing Commander Peter Ayerst, DFC

Peter Ayerst in France, whilst flying Hurricanes with 73 Squadron in March 1940.

I had been in France flying Hurricanes from the beginning of World War II until June 1940, with No. 73 Squadron, until the squadron returned to the UK. I was then posted to a Spitfire Operational Training Unit at Hawarden, near Chester, as an Instructor, where I flew Spitfires for the first time. They were wonderful looking aircraft and equally wonderful to fly.

After my period of instructing I joined a new Spitfire Squadron as a Flight Commander and helped train new pilots to the Squadron. The Squadron was equipped with Mark VB Spitfires.

Then I was one of twenty fighter pilots who were selected to go to North Africa and join Hurricane squadrons of the Desert Air Force, prior to the Battle of Alamein. After two years of very intensive operational flying I returned to the UK and went back on Spitfires again.

In April 1944 I joined No. 124 (Baroda) Squadron as a Flight Commander. The Squadron was equipped with high altitude MK VII Spitfires. We were patrolling at high altitude over all the Channel Port areas prior to and after 'D' Day on 6 June 1944. Eventually, by mid July 1944, the Allied ground forces had advanced to Belgium and beyond and there was no need to patrol the Channel Ports any longer and No. 124 Squadron was re-equipped with the Spitfire MK IXE. Our role changed from high altitude patrols to lower level operations, including Arnhem and close escorts to our Bomber aircraft who were bombing V1 launch sites and many targets to help the ground forces, such as German fuel dumps and troop concentrations. We then had long-range fuel tanks fitted to our Spitfires and escorted Halifaxes and Lancasters, when in mid 1944 they started doing daylight bombing attacks in support of

Peter Ayerst at RAF Manston in 1944.

Above right: Peter Ayerst with his great friend, the late Alex Henshaw. In January 1945, Peter became a Test Pilot at the Vickers Armstrong Aircraft factory at Castle Bromwich, and the Chief Test Pilot at the factory was Alex Henshaw.

Far right: Peter Ayerst at Duxford recently with Spitfire Mk. VB, JH-C, BM597.

the Allied Armies. During this period we escorted HM King George VI from Northolt to Eindhoven.

Then at the end of January 1945 my tour with No. 124 Squadron had come to an end and I was posted to Vickers Armstrong's Aircraft factory at Castle Bromwich, near Birmingham, as a Test Pilot. At this time it was the biggest aircraft factory in the country and employed 25,000 people at the one location; at the peak rate of production they were producing 320 Spitfires per month plus 30 Lancasters. The Chief Test Pilot was Alex Henshaw, the well-known aviator who in early 1939 flew a Mew Gull to Cape Town and back in four and a half days.

At this stage of my flying career I had flown 13 different types of Spitfire, the latest one being the Mark 22, which was fitted with the Rolls-Royce Griffon engine. The Mark 22 Spitfire was not made in time for World War II but nevertheless was a very formidable aircraft with a very high performance. I carried out 162 test flights on the Mark 22.

THE year 1931 saw the Supermarine Aircraft Company at Southampton and its Chief Designer Reginald Mitchell firmly established as world-leaders in the design and production of high-speed racing seaplanes. That September a Supermarine S.6B won the coveted Schneider Trophy outright for Britain with a flight round the circular course at an average speed of 340 mph. Later, a sister aircraft raised the world's absolute speed record to 379 mph. And at the end of the month an S.6B with a modified Rolls-Royce R 27 engine again raised the absolute air speed record, to 407 mph.

Brilliant though these floatplanes undoubtedly were, they had been tailor-made to perform just one task – that of achieving the highest possible speed. Nothing else mattered. They were strictly 'this-side-up, handle-with-care machines' with a very short endurance and poor manoeuvrability. Moreover, in the nature of things, the demand for such aircraft was strictly limited.

Also in the autumn of 1931, the Air Ministry in London issued Specification F.7/30 for a new type of aircraft to equip its fighter squadrons. At that time the fastest aircraft in RAF service was the Hawker Fury biplane with a maximum speed of 207 mph. It was, therefore, little more than half as fast as the Supermarine S.6B during its final record-breaking run. The F.7/30 specification laid down the following requirements for the new fighter. It had to have:

- the highest possible rate of climb
- the highest possible speed above 15,000 ft
- a good view for the pilot particularly during combat
- good manoeuvrability
- be capable of easy and rapid production in quantity
- ease of maintenance
- an armament of four .303 inch machine guns and provision to carry four 20 lb bombs.

At the time the specification was issued Great Britain was in the middle of a financial slump and times were hard for the nation's aircraft industry. As a result there was intense competition to secure what might be a lucrative order from the RAF and possibly foreign governments as well. Seven aircraft companies designed and built eight fighter prototypes for the F.7/30 competition. Five of the aircraft were biplanes and the other three were monoplanes.

The Supermarine submission was a monoplane, the Type 224, which first flew in February 1934. Power was supplied by a Rolls-Royce Goshawk engine developing 660 hp, which was the most powerful British engine then available for installation in fighters. The Type 224 had a top speed of 238 mph and it took 8 minutes to climb to 15,000 ft.

A major problem afflicting the Type 224 concerned the complex system of cooling employed by the Goshawk engine. To avoid the drag penalty resulting from use of an external radiator the new fighter employed an evaporative cooling system. After the water coolant had

"When I joined Supermarine the design of the Type 224 was virtually complete and I had little to do with it. As is now well known, that fighter was not successful. My own personal feeling is that the design team had done so well with the S.5 and the S.6 racing floatplanes, which in the end reached speeds of over 400 mph, that they thought it would be child's play to design a fighter intended to fly at little over half that speed. They never made that mistake again."

Following rejection of the Type 224 the Supermarine design team began work on a more effective fighter. On the 660 hp from the Goshawk engine no aircraft was likely to exceed 250 mph by much. But towards the end of 1934 Rolls Royce had a much better engine in prospect. The company's new 27 litre V-12 engine designated PV12 (later named Merlin) passed its 100-hour type test when it developed 790 hp at 12,000 ft with an eventual planned target output of 1,000 hp. That offered the prospect of reaching speeds well in excess of 300 mph.

Left: Close-up of the Type 224, showing the 'chunky' nature of the construction. The fighter had a mediocre performance and was not selected for production.

The Gloster SS37 won the F.7/30 fighter design competition. In horizontal flight this biplane was 4 mph faster than the Type 224. It was more manoeuvrable, however, and in the combat climb to 15,000 ft it reached that altitude in 1.5 minutes less than Type 224. With some changes the SS37 entered service in the RAF as the Gladiator, the last biplane fighter to see service in the RAF.

passed through the engine it emerged as steam to be pumped through to the internal radiators built into the leading edge of each wing. There the steam should have condensed so that the resultant hot water could be pumped back to the engine. The system often failed to perform as intended. Flt Lt (later Grp Capt) Hugh Wilson flew the Type 224 a few times but he did not find it an enjoyable experience:

"The engine used to overheat almost all the time. We were told that when the red light came on in the cockpit the engine was overheating. But the trouble was that just about every time you took off the red light came on. It seemed the engine was always overheating."

The Type 224 was not a refined design either structurally or aerodynamically and it did not show up well against its competitors. The winner of the F.7/30 competition was a biplane of conventional layout, the Gloster SS.37. It had a maximum speed of 242 mph, making it a little faster than the Type 224. But the Gloster fighter possessed a superb rate of climb and it reached 15,000 ft in 6.5 minutes – 1.5 minutes ahead of Supermarine's offering. With some modifications the SS37 would enter RAF service as the Gladiator.

Beverley Shenstone joined the Supermarine design team as an aerodynamicist in 1934. During a discussion of the Type 224 with the author he commented:

In November 1934 the board of Vickers, Supermarine's parent company, allocated funds for Mitchell and his team to design a new fighter powered by the PV12 engine. The proposed machine aroused immediate interest at the Air Ministry, and in the following month the company received a £10,000 contract to build a prototype fighter to Mitchell's proposed 'improved F.7/30' design. The new fighter received the designation F.37/34.

The overwhelming credit for the fighter that now took shape in the drawing office at Woolston must of course go to Mitchell and his small design team as well as the Rolls-Royce engineers at Derby struggling to improve the power output and reliability of the PV12 engine. But others, working for the government, also deserve a share of the credit.

The F.7/30 Specification had called for an armament of four rifle-calibre machine guns, which seemed a useful increase in firepower compared with the two carried by RAF fighter types in the early 1930s. But the primary role of the F.7/30 fighter was that of bomber destroyer and Sqn Ldr Ralph Sorley, working at the Operational Requirements section at the Air Ministry, had doubts on that score. He argued that the relatively slow-firing Vickers .303 inch machine gun, which fired at a rate of 850 rounds per minute and equipped all RAF fighters at that time, lacked the necessary punch. He reasoned that four of these guns would be insufficient to destroy the fast all-metal bombers that would soon enter service. An experienced pilot himself, Sorley believed it would be extremely difficult for a pilot to hold his gun sight on a high-speed bomber for more than about 2 seconds. So, unless the lethal blow could be administered in that time, the bomber would escape. Sorley later wrote:

"By 1934 a new Browning gun was at last being tested in Britain which offered a higher rate of fire [1,100 rounds per minute]. After much arithmetic, I reached the answer of eight [Browning guns] as being the number required to give a lethal dose in 2 seconds. I reckoned that the bomber's speed would probably be such as to allow the pursuing fighter only one chance of attack, so it must be destroyed in that vital 2 second burst."

Sorley's carefully-reasoned arguments convinced the Deputy Chief of the Air Staff, Air Vice-Marshal Edgar Ludlow-Hewitt, that the new fighter should carry eight Browning guns. In April 1935 Sorley visited the Supermarine works to discuss the possibility of fitting the revised armament into the new fighter. Mitchell assured the RAF officer that it would indeed be possible to fit the extra four guns into the fighter's wings.

Jack Davis, working in the Supermarine drawing office, was given the task of redesigning the wing to take the extra four guns. He recalled:

"It did not take me long to work out where the guns had to go. The rib positions had all been decided so it was just a question of fitting the guns in between them. But as one went further out the wing became thinner and the ammunition boxes had to be longer to accommodate the 300 rounds required for each gun. That meant the outer guns had to be quite a long way out. In fact, to get them into the wing, I had to design very shallow blisters to fit around them. The aerodynamics people did not like the idea but they accepted it: there was no alternative if we were to get the eight guns in without redesigning the entire wing."

By mid-1935 the design of the F.37/34 had largely been settled except for one important aspect: how to cool the PV12 engine. The initial thought was to employ the evaporative cooling system, even though this had performed miserably on the Type 224. The likely alternative, a conventional cooling system employing an external radiator, would add considerably to the drag and would reduce the fighter's maximum speed.

The provision of an effective method for cooling the engine was no trivial matter. When the PV12 ran at full power it produced the heat equivalent of four hundred one-Kw electric fires running simultaneously. Unless that heat was dissipated the engine would overheat and suffer damage. The solution came from Fred Meredith, a scientist working at the Royal Aircraft Establishment at Farnborough. He had been conducting experiments with a new type of ducted radiator in which the airflow entered a duct at the front. Its cross-sectional area was progressively narrowed which reduced the velocity of the air and increased its pressure. The air then passed through the radiator matrix, where it picked up the heat and expanded. The heated air then passed through a divergent duct at the rear. The ducted radiator therefore acted rather like a low-powered ramjet engine: the air entered the duct and was compressed, it then passed through the radiator matrix and was heated and finally emerged from the rear of the duct with a slightly increased velocity.

The system produced relatively little thrust, but by removing a potential source of drag it brought a considerable advantage. Reginald

A VERY TALENTED AIRCRAFT DESIGNER

Reginald Joseph Mitchell was born on 20 May 1895 at Talke near Stoke on Trent, the first of the five children of schoolmaster Herbert Mitchell. In 1911, aged 16, he left school and became an apprentice at a Stoke engineering firm manufacturing steam locomotives. His heart was in aviation, however, and in 1916 aged 21 he moved to Pemberton Billing Ltd at its works at Woolston near Southampton. That company was engaged in the repair of aircraft for the Admiralty and in 1918 it was renamed Supermarine Aviation Ltd.

The young Mitchell advanced rapidly in the company and in 1919, still aged only 24, his talents brought their due recognition and he was appointed chief designer. During the 1920s Supermarine concentrated on the design and production of seaplanes. The company first achieved prominence in 1922 when its Sea Lion biplane flying boat won the Schneider Trophy contest by rounding the circuit at an average speed of 145 mph. In the years to come Mitchell did not rest on his laurels.

Reginald Mitchell, chief designer.

Three years later, in 1925, his Supermarine S.4 monoplane floatplane gained the world speed record for floatplanes at 226 mph. Two years later his S.5 won the Schneider Trophy when it completed the course at an average speed of 281 mph.

In 1925 the twin-engined Southampton reconnaissance flying boat appeared. It was Mitchell's first design to gain a substantial production order. The RAF bought 68 of these machines in what was then considered a huge order. A number of foreign governments purchased a further 16 of these aircraft.

In 1928 Vickers Aviation purchased Supermarine but the Southampton-based company retained its identity and Mitchell continued as chief designer. The company's line of small racing seaplanes continued to score successes, its S.6B winning the Schneider Trophy outright for Britain and breaking the absolute speed record. For his part Reginald Mitchell still had youth on his side – he had yet to celebrate his 37th birthday.

Jeffrey Quill rose to become chief test pilot at Supermarine.

Mitchell knew a good idea when he saw one, and he redesigned his fighter to carry a Meredith-type ducted radiator under the starboard wing. With the 990 hp available from the latest version of the Merlin (as the engine had now been named) it was predicted that the new fighter would attain a maximum speed of around 350 mph.

Towards the end of February 1936 the assembly of the new fighter was completed. At that time most major air forces – the RAF included – operated fabric-covered biplane fighters with open cockpits and fixed undercarriages. Compared with them the new Supermarine fighter was a revelation: a cantilever monoplane constructed almost entirely of metal, with an enclosed cockpit and a retractable undercarriage.

The fighter was wheeled on to the hardstanding beside the Woolston works for engine running and system checks. Then it was dismantled and transported by road to the nearby airfield at Eastleigh, now Southampton Airport. Early in March, following reassembly, the fighter underwent further engine runs and checks. When they were completed an official from the Aeronautical Inspection Directorate made a detailed examination of the aircraft and pronounced it fit to fly.

SOME OF THE MEN WHO CREATED THE SPITFIRE ALONGSIDE REGINALD MITCHELL

Joseph Smith, chief draughtsman, became chief designer after Mitchell's death.

Beverley Shenstone, aerodynamicist.

Alan Clifton, head of the technical office.

Victor Bibire did the stress calculations.

Wilfred Hennessy also undertook stress calculations.

Above: The technical office at Woolston where the weight, stress and performance calculations of the new fighter were made.

Right: The drawing office at Woolston where the fighter took shape.

ON the afternoon of 5 March 1936 the Supermarine F.37/34 fighter serial number K5054 was made ready for its maiden flight. For reasons now lost in time that first flight lasted only 8 min. Vickers' chief test pilot, Capt J 'Mutt' Summers, then returned to Eastleigh (see text box, page 16).

For the maiden flight the fighter was fitted with a fine pitch propeller to provide optimum performance at the low-speed end of the performance envelope. On the following day, 6 March, Summers took the fighter on its second flight. For this the aircraft was fitted with a coarse pitch propeller, to enable it to reach higher speeds.

Shortly afterwards the Vickers parent company bestowed a name on its new fighter aircraft: Spitfire. By all accounts, Reginald Mitchell was not enthralled with the choice. Jeffrey Quill heard him comment: "It's the sort of bloody silly name they would give it."

During its early flight tests the Spitfire clocked up a maximum speed of around 330 mph. That was good but it was not good enough. The 20 mph shortfall placed the Supermarine fighter's maximum speed uncomfortably close to the 315 mph attained by its competitor for an RAF order, the Hawker Hurricane. The Hawker fighter was larger and less refined than the Spitfire and – an important point to consider when dealing with the ever-parsimonious British Treasury – it was also cheaper to build. That prompted the obvious question: was the extra expense of producing the Spitfire worth the extra 15 mph? Engineers at Supermarine traced the cause of the speed loss to the type of propeller fitted to the aircraft. Several types

Left and right: The prototype Supermarine F.37/34, serial number K5054, pictured at Eastleigh airfield (now Southampton Airport) shortly before its maiden flight on 5 March 1936. For this flight the metal parts of the aircraft were left unpainted while the fabric control surfaces were doped. The aircraft carried no radio or armament (though gun ports were fitted), the undercarriage was locked in the down position and it was fitted with a fine pitch propeller to optimise take-off performance. The Rolls-Royce car in the background to the photograph at right was R.J. Mitchell's.

Maiden flight

On the morning of 5 March 1936, K5054 was wheeled on to the airfield at Eastleigh. Later that day 'Mutt' Summers prepared to take the fighter into the air. After brief preliminaries he climbed into the cockpit, strapped in and started the engine. When he was satisfied that all was as it should be, he waved the chocks away. He gave a burst of power to get the little fighter moving across the grass as he sought to get the 'feel' of the controls before taking off. Jeffrey Quill witnessed the scene together with Reginald Mitchell, most of the design team and company workers at the airfield. Quill recalled:

"Mutt taxied around for a bit then, without too much in the way of preliminaries, went over to the far side of the airfield, turned into wind and took off. With the fine pitch prop the new fighter fairly leapt off the ground and climbed away. It then passed out of our sight but I know what Mutt would have been doing. First, he would have needed to confirm that the technical people had worked out the stalling speed correctly so he could get back on the ground safely. To that end he would have taken it to a safe altitude, about 5,000 ft, and tried a dummy landing to find the best approach speed and make sure that when it stalled, the aircraft did not flick on to its back or do anything unpleasant like that. Probably Mutt did a few steep turns to try out the controls. Then, having checked that everything really important was all right, he landed and taxied in."

Despite lasting only 8 minutes the flight was sufficient to show that the aircraft had no unpleasant characteristics.

K5054 pictured in the hangar at Eastleigh after it had been painted in the company's trademark light blue colour scheme.

were tested and, using the best of them, the Spitfire reached 348 mph to place it well ahead of its Hawker rival.

On 26 May Summers delivered the Spitfire prototype to the RAF test establishment at Martlesham Heath where experienced service pilots conducted their own independent evaluation of the aircraft's performance. That led to a small but unexpected bonus. The Martlesham tests measured the Spitfire's maximum speed at 349 mph at 16,800 ft, 1 mph above Supermarine's figure.

For the Royal Air Force the new fighter had appeared at exactly the right time. In Germany the newly-formed *Luftwaffe* was being built up rapidly and its own high-performance all-metal monoplane fighter, the Messerschmitt Bf 109, was about to enter large-scale production. To meet this potential threat the British Government signed a contract for 310 Spitfires in June 1936.

The test programme at Martlesham Heath continued until 1 August when the prototype returned to Eastleigh for the installation of military equipment. This included the eight .303 inch Browning machine guns as well as a reflector sight and a radio. Several minor modifications were also incorporated which included a new oil cooler, the installation of a spin recovery parachute and the latest version of the Merlin engine which now developed an extra 60 hp.

Testing the new fighter resumed early in December 1936. The first item on the agenda was to test its ability to recover from spins as the centre of gravity was moved progressively rearwards. It was feared that the aircraft might enter a flat spin and fail to recover using the usual stick-forwards-and-opposite-rudder technique. To avoid that possibility the Spitfire featured a makeshift spin recovery system. Jeffrey Quill, by then in charge of testing the fighter, told the author:

"The small parachute, about 3 ft in diameter, was folded and housed in a box about 9 in by 6 in by 2 in and fitted in the cockpit on the right-hand side. From the parachute a steel cable ran out

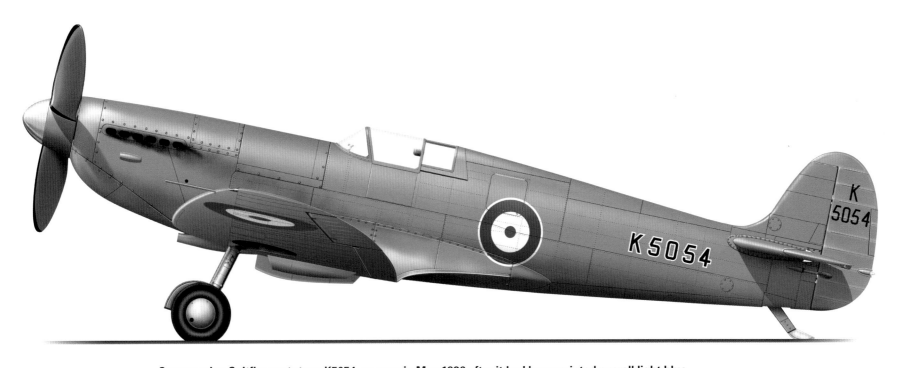

Supermarine Spitfire prototype K5054, as seen in May 1936 after it had been painted overall light blue.

K5054 taxies in at Eastleigh after a test flight. Note the black stain spreading rearwards from the engine's exhaust stubs, which may indicate full throttle runs had been undertaken. Note also the redesigned fin and rudder as against that first seen on the prototype on roll-out.

between the front of the canopy and the windscreen, then to the base of the fin where it was attached to a ringbolt. To stop it flapping about in the airflow, the cable was held down at regular intervals with sticky tape. If the aircraft got into a flat spin and would not come out using the normal recovery procedure, the idea was that I should slide back the canopy, grab the folded parachute and toss it out on the side opposite to the direction of the spin – taking care not to let the cable pass across my neck if the parachute had to be tossed to the left. The parachute would then stream out behind the tail and as it opened would yank the aircraft straight, thereby providing what was in effect a much more powerful rudder. Once the parachute had pulled the aircraft straight, it could be jettisoned."

Quill tested the parachute and jettison system on 11 December. The arrangement worked as intended. In the following days the fighter flew seven times, with the centre of gravity moved progressively aft between each flight. He put the fighter into a spin in either direction. Each time it recovered normally without resort to the use of the parachute.

Early in 1937 Reginald Mitchell was diagnosed as suffering from cancer. The treatment he received failed to relieve his condition and

Calibrating the air speed indicator

During the final week of March 1936, Supermarine test pilots Jeffrey Quill and George Pickering took over the testing of K5054. Their first move was to calibrate the airspeed indicator to correct it for possible errors. Jeffrey Quill described the process:

"These trials had to be flown early in the morning because we had to have completely still air. We needed a straight measured course so we used a section of the Portsmouth to Eastleigh railway line between two bridges. On each bridge we stationed a man with a stopwatch and a field telephone. Then I had to fly the aeroplane along the course very accurately, first at 100 mph indicated, then back at 120, and so on up to the maximum speed of the aircraft. From the readings taken by the men on the ground, we could work out the position errors and correct for them in our other test work."

in June of that year he died at the tragically young age of 42. But by then Mitchell's legacy to the nation, potentially the world's

THE ROLLS-ROYCE MERLIN

If there was one other single ingredient in the success of the Spitfire, it would have to be the Rolls-Royce Merlin aero engine. For without this engine and its subsequent derivatives the aircraft would not have been the success it was.

The Merlin is a liquid-cooled, 27 litre (1,650 cu in) capacity, V-12 piston aero engine, designed and built by Rolls-Royce Limited. Rolls-Royce named the engine the Merlin after a small European falcon (Falco columbarius). This followed the company convention of naming its piston aero engines after birds of prey.

First run in 1933 and initially known as the PV12, a series of rapidly applied developments, brought about by wartime needs, improved performance markedly.

One of the most notable developments was in the area of supercharging with the introduction of the Two-stage, two-speed unit first seen in the Spitfire Mk IX, one of the most successful of Spitfire variants.

Some 14 different variants of the Merlin were developed – with production being undertaken in the UK and under licence in the US by Packard.

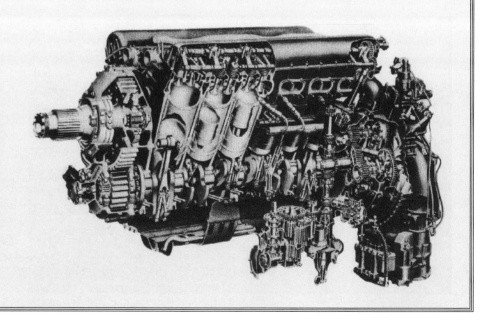

A by now fully-armed K5054, pictured in the standard RAF Dark Green and Dark Earth camouflage scheme applied in September 1937. Note the very tall radio mast and the fitting of ejector exhausts.

most effective fighter, had proved its capabilities beyond reasonable doubt.

The word 'potentially' is appropriate because the series of tests revealed that the prototype Spitfire had a major shortcoming. At low and medium altitude all eight machine guns had successfully fired all 300 rounds of ammunition over the North Sea. Then, in March 1937, an RAF pilot took the fighter to 32,000 ft for a high-altitude firing test. It ended in fiasco. One gun fired 171 rounds, another fired eight, and yet another fired four, while the remaining five guns failed to fire at all. That was bad enough but as the fighter landed the jolt released the breechblocks of three guns that had not fired and each loosed off a round in the general direction of Felixstowe!

The cause of the problem was that the guns had frozen up at high altitude. The solution was to fit a duct to convey hot air from the engine coolant radiator to the gun bays. Getting that solution to work was no easy matter. In July 1938 the problem still persisted and the first production Spitfires were about to be delivered to the RAF. That led the Chief of the Air Staff, Marshal of the Royal Air Force Sir Cyril Newall, to comment during a secret meeting of the Air Council: "If the guns will not fire at the heights at which the Spitfires are likely to encounter enemy bombers, they will be useless as fighting aircraft."

The problem of guns freezing up persisted until October 1938 when, following a series of modifications, all eight fired off all their ammunition at high altitude. Subsequent production Spitfires incorporated the design changes, which were applied retrospectively to earlier aircraft.

During the early summer of 1938 production Spitfires began to emerge in growing numbers from the Supermarine assembly hangar at Eastleigh. The prototype's part in the test programme came to an end. The hand-built prototype differed greatly from production aircraft and it was sent to Farnborough where it served as a high-speed 'hack' to test various new features.

On 4 September 1939, the day after Great Britain declared war on Germany, the prototype suffered serious damage in a fatal landing accident at Farnborough. That was in the days before the desire to preserve historic aircraft. The Spitfire prototype could have been repaired but nobody in a position of authority thought it worth the effort. It was scrapped. The prototype had cost the British taxpayer £15,776. Rarely has public money been better spent.

The now camouflaged K5054 pictured in flight.

High altitude shock

The Spitfire's high performance enabled it to reach altitudes rarely visited before. On 11 July 1936 Flt Lt (later Air Marshal Sir) Humphrey Edwards Jones took the prototype Spitfire up as high as it would go. A climb lasting 37 minutes took him to 34,700 ft. He told the author:

"In those days that was very high. It was the first time I had ever left a condensation trail or seen one. I was horrified. I didn't know what was happening: all that smoke coming out of the engine exhausts."

After a careful check of his instruments the pilot ascertained that the strange phenomenon, whatever caused it, was benign. As he descended, the smoke trail disappeared. The manifestation would be the subject of considerable discussion after Edwards Jones landed at Martlesham Heath.

The instrument panel of K5054 showing the initial layout, which was revised for production aircraft. The large instrument, top centre, is an altimeter and the vertical 'rod and ball' lever in the far right of the cockpit is for undercarriage retraction.

3 SPITFIRE INTO SERVICE

Left: K9787, the first production Spitfire.

THE first production Spitfire flew in May 1938 and in August No 19 Squadron at Duxford received its first examples. Sqn Ldr (later Air Cdre) Henry Cozens, the unit's commander, recalled his impressions during his first flight in the new fighter:

"After flying the [Gloster] Gauntlet, my first impression of the Spitfire was that its acceleration seemed rather slow and the controls were a lot heavier than I had expected. Thinking about it afterwards, I realised why: the Gauntlet took off at about 70 mph and was flat out at about 220 mph; the Spitfire took off at about the same speed but could do well over 350 mph. In other words, the speed range was far greater and although the acceleration [in the Spitfire] was in fact greater, it took somewhat longer to reach its maximum speed. Moreover, as it neared the top end of the speed range the Spitfire's controls became beautifully light."

Henry Cozens went on to list some of the shortcomings, all relatively minor, that afflicted these early production aircraft.

"For one thing the engines of these first Spitfires were difficult to start: the low-geared electric starter rotated the propeller blades so slowly that when the cylinder fired there was usually insufficient push to flick the engine round to fire the next. There would be a 'puff' noise, then the propeller would resume turning on the starter."

Other problems centred on the engines leaking oil and pilots grazing their knuckles on the side of the cockpit when manually pumping the hydraulic system to raise the undercarriage. Also, the taller pilots had insufficient headroom when the cockpit canopy was shut.

Engineers at Supermarine and Rolls-Royce devised modifications to cure these problems. With a more powerful starter motor, the engine-starting problem was overcome. A redesigned bulged cockpit canopy provided extra headroom for pilots. An engine-driven hydraulic system to raise and lower the undercarriage removed the need for a hand pump. These improvements were easy enough to introduce. However, the problem of the oil leaks, although gradually reduced, would remain with the Merlin engine throughout its long career.

By October 1938 Spitfire production was running at 13 aircraft per month. The new aircraft coming off the production line carried an effective gun heating system which enabled them to fire their weapons at high altitude.

When the Second World War began the RAF had taken delivery of 306 Spitfires. Of these, 187 formed the equipment of 11 Fighter Command squadrons, 71 were held at maintenance units ready for issue to replace losses, and 12 served with trials units or were engaged in other second-line tasks. The remaining 36 machines had been written off in accidents.

At the same time the Spitfire underwent numerous modifications to improve its fighting capability. A thick slab of laminated glass fixed in front of the windscreen protected the pilot from projectiles fired from ahead. For further protection, steel sheets weighing 75 lbs were

The first Spitfire written off was K9792, which suffered a fractured axle stub during landing. The pilot, Plt Off G Sinclair, was unhurt.

Spitfires of No 19 Squadron practise formation flying early in 1939.

Spitfires of No 19 Squadron lined up at Duxford in readiness for the station's press day on 4 May 1939. The dog which joined the parade belonged to the unit's commander, Sqn Ldr Henry Cozens.

installed behind and beneath the pilot's seat. Another important addition was the installation of an IFF (Identification Friend or Foe) transponder. This transmitted a coded signal which identified the aircraft as 'friendly' on British ground radar stations.

The Spitfires in the initial production batch had two-bladed fixed-pitch wooden airscrews. On subsequent aircraft they were replaced by three-bladed two-pitch metal airscrews. The fine pitch setting was for use at lower speeds with a coarse pitch setting for use at higher speeds. In the spring of 1940 the two-pitch propellers in their turn were replaced by constant-speed three-bladed metal airscrews. In flight the constant-speed drive unit continually adjusted the pitch of the blades, allowing the propeller to operate at its optimum rpm setting for the combination of boost and airspeed selected by the pilot. This new propeller brought about an impressive improvement in the fighter's rate of climb, clipping 3.5 minutes off the time taken to reach 20,000 ft.

A further improvement in performance came with the use of 100-octane petrol imported from the USA to replace the 87-octane fuel previously used. At altitudes below the full throttle height of 16,500 ft, the new fuel allowed supercharger boost to be increased from plus 6.5 pounds to plus 12 pounds for a maximum of five minutes in combat. That increased the Spitfire's maximum speed at sea level by 25 mph and at 10,000 ft by 34 mph. At all altitudes up to full-throttle height, the fighter's climbing performance was also significantly improved.

In aviation it is rare to get something for nothing. The modifications added about 335 lbs to the Spitfire's all-up weight, taking it to around 6,155 lbs. Some also increased drag. For example, the toughened glass slab in front of the windscreen shaved 6 mph off the maximum speed, while the wire aerials for the IFF equipment cost another 2 mph. The maximum speed usually quoted for the Spitfire I is 362 mph at 18,500 ft. But in fact that figure referred to the first production aircraft during its performance testing in 1938. In the spring of 1940 the maximum speed of a fully-modified Spitfire

Spitfires and Hurricanes from several units lined up on the airfield at Digby, Lincolnshire. The occasion was a massed fly-past over Midlands cities to publicise Empire Air Day on 20 May 1939 and boost civilian morale as war clouds gathered.

Below: Spitfire of No 66 Squadron, the second unit to re-equip with the type. The object above the starboard wing root is a gun camera.

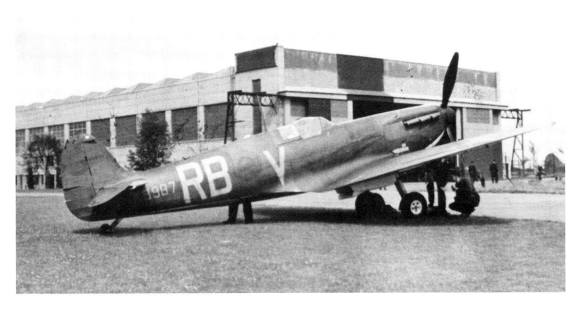

was about 350 mph at the same altitude. And it was in that condition that the aircraft received its initial baptism of fire.

The so-called 'Phoney War' during which the Spitfire squadrons saw relatively little action lasted from September 1939 to May 1940. In that seven-month period the size of the Spitfire force doubled, from ten squadrons to 20, and all units underwent a programme of intensive training.

That relatively quiet phase of the conflict came to an abrupt end on 10 May 1940 when German forces launched their powerful *Blitzkrieg* offensives into Holland, Belgium and France. Within two weeks the Allied ground forces had been severed in two, with the northern part forced to withdraw into a narrowing pocket that hinged on the French port of Dunkirk. During the final week of May the Royal Navy launched a full-scale evacuation to bring these troops back to England. RAF Fighter Command mounted an all-out effort to cover the evacuation. For the first time the Spitfire went into action against its German equivalent, the formidable Messerschmitt Bf 109. Now Reginald Mitchell's little fighter was able to demonstrate that it could take punishment as well as dish it out.

With friends like that, who needs enemies? During a practice formation flight in March 1940, Plt Off Wilfred Clouston suffered the loss of much of his rudder and elevators caused by the propeller of his wingman's aircraft. In a demonstration of skilful flying, he made a belly landing on Newmarket race course with little further damage to the aircraft.

Large-scale production of Spitfire wings at Supermarine's Woolston factory photographed early in 1939.

Spitfire K9791, the fifth production aircraft, was retained by Supermarine to test new modifications. The machine is seen here fitted with a three-bladed constant-speed airscrew.

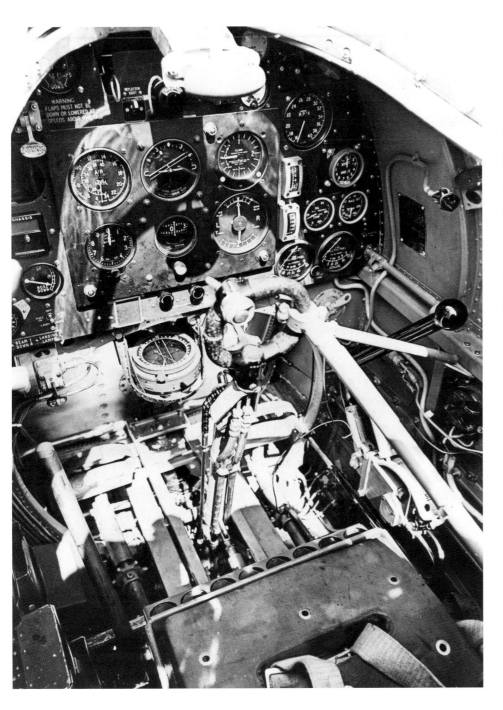

K9791 tested with a plywood mock-up installation of an extra fuel tank under each wing. The modification was not taken further.

Close-up of the GM2 gun sight fitted to Spitfires.

Cockpit of an early production Spitfire I.

Close shave over Dunkirk

During an action over Dunkirk on 25 May Plt Off Colin Gray, a New Zealander flying Spitfires with No 54 Squadron, engaged a Bf 109 and watched it go down. He then committed the fundamental blunder for a combat pilot of concentrating his attention on his victim to the exclusion of all else. That mistake nearly cost him his life:

"Suddenly there was one hell of a row, like somebody running a bar along a piece of corrugated iron. The stick was knocked out of my hand and ended up in the left-hand corner of the cockpit and my aircraft flicked into a spiral dive. I grabbed the stick and hauled back on it. The Spitfire responded immediately and started to climb. I looked behind but didn't see anyone. The German pilot had not repeated the mistake of following me down. I selected 12 lbs [emergency] boost and continued my climb. The airspeed indicator read 240 mph and I thought: 'This is bloody marvellous.' [The normal maximum speed for a Spitfire in a steep climb was about 190 mph indicated]. *But then, as I continued the climb, the Spitfire began to shudder and it seemed as if it was going to stall. I couldn't understand it, the airspeed indicator still read 240 mph. I eased the stick forwards but still it read 240 mph. Then I realised: my pitot head had been shot away and the needle had dropped to the 240 mph position on the dial under gravity.*

"I levelled out and took stock of the situation. One cannon shell had gone through the port aileron. That was what had knocked the stick out of my hand and sent the aircraft into the violent spiral dive which shook off the Messerschmitt. The airspeed indicator was out and there was no air pressure or hydraulic pressure. That meant I had no flaps or brakes and I couldn't lower the undercarriage using the main hydraulic system. As I approached Hornchurch I blew down the undercarriage using the emergency carbon dioxide system.

"The landing was very difficult. With the flaps up one came in at a different attitude than usual and, of course, I had no idea of my airspeed – the indicator still read 240 mph. The first time I came in too fast. The station commander at Hornchurch, Wg Cdr 'Daddy' Bouchier, was watching my performance and was overheard to say: 'The silly young bugger, he's going too fast. He'll never get in.' He was right. I got my wheels almost on the ground, realised I wasn't going to make it and took off again. The second time I stood well back from the airfield and dragged the aircraft in at just above stalling speed. That time I landed and as I touched down the elevator cable finally parted and the control column collapsed into my stomach.

"On examination of the Spitfire afterwards it was found that a cannon shell had gone through the inspection hatch in the rear fuselage and exploded inside. Splinters from the shell had slashed their way out of the skinning, leaving it looking like a cheese grater. The air bottles had been knocked out and so were the batteries. There were bullet holes up and down the fuselage and, of course, the cannon shell through the aileron. From the entry and exit holes of the bullets it was clear the Messerschmitt had dived on me from the right and above. It had been a very neat piece of deflection shooting. 'The Spitfire was put up on trestles and people from Vickers were invited to come and look at it to see how much it had suffered. It was the first Hornchurch aircraft that had been fairly well clobbered and still got back. Soon there would be many others."

Colin Gray went on to attain the rank of wing commander and ended the war credited with 27.5 aerial victories. He never forgot the lesson of the action on 25 May 1940 when his lack of experience nearly brought a precipitate end to his career as a fighter pilot.

Close-up of the bulged canopy and laminated glass windscreen fitted as standard on Spitfires early in the war.

Spitfires engaged Messerschmitt 109s in large numbers for the first time during the Dunkirk evacuation in May and early June 1940. On 2 June Plt Off O Pigg of No 72 Squadron engaged Messerschmitt 109s over the port and his Spitfire sustained several hits. The pilot made a wheels-up landing near Gravesend and escaped without serious injury.

The 600th production Spitfire pictured in April 1940 during its production test flight with Jeffrey Quill at the controls. This aircraft served with No 64 Squadron during the Battle of Britain.

Spitfires of No 41 Squadron pictured with Armstrong Whitworth Ensign transport aircraft during a deployment exercise early in the war.

Above: The Messerschmitt Bf 109 E proved a worthy opponent for the Spitfire during the hard fought air actions of 1940.

Spitfire I of No 72 Squadron displaying the SD code letters worn by this unit during 1939 and the early months of 1940.

Right: One of the few Messerschmitt Bf 109 Es that fell into the hands of the French forces during the Battle of France and was subsequently tested by the French and the British. The aircraft seen here from JG 54 has had its Luftwaffe markings overpainted with French colours.

SPITFIRE MK 1 VERSUS MESSERSCHMITT BF 109 E

In November 1939 a Messerschmitt Bf 109 E was forced down in France and captured intact. After testing in France, the aircraft went to the Royal Aircraft Establishment at Farnborough for comparative trials against the Spitfire I. Following the trial, the Air Tactics Branch of the Air Ministry issued the following report on the comparative fighting trial between the Bf 109 and a Spitfire.

1. *The trial commenced with the two aircraft taking off together, with the Spitfire slightly behind and using plus-6 lb boost and 3,000 rpm.*

2. *When fully airborne, the pilot of the Spitfire reduced his engine revolutions to 2,650 rpm and was then able to overtake and out-climb the Me 109. At 4,000 ft the Spitfire pilot was 1,000 ft above the Me 109, from which position he was able to get on to its tail and remain there within effective range despite all efforts of the pilot of the Me 109 to shake him off.*

3. *The Spitfire then allowed the Me 109 to get on to his tail and attempted to shake him off. This he found quite easy owing to the superior manoeuvrability of his aircraft, particularly in the looping plane and at low speeds between 100 and 140 mph. By executing a steep turn just above stalling speed, he ultimately got back into a position on the tail of the Me 109.*

4. *Another effective form of evasion with the Spitfire was found to be a steep, climbing spiral at 120 mph, using plus-6 lb boost and 2,650 rpm; in this manoeuvre the Spitfire gained rapidly on the Me 109, eventually allowing the pilot to execute a half roll on to the tail of his opponent.*

5. *Comparative speed trials were then carried out, and the Spitfire proved to be considerably the faster of the two, both in acceleration and straight and level flight, without having to make use of the emergency plus-12 lbs boost. During diving trials, the Spitfire pilot found that by engaging fully coarse pitch and using plus-2 lbs of boost, his aircraft was superior to the Me 109.*

The Farnborough trial proved to the satisfaction of all that the Spitfire I was greatly superior to the Messerschmitt 109 E at altitudes around 4,000 ft. The captured Messerschmitt suffered difficulties with its engine cooling system and as a result it failed to demonstrate the fact that it could out-climb the Spitfire at most altitudes. Moreover, *Luftwaffe* pilots had learned in Spain the folly of getting drawn into a low speed turning contest when engaging a more manoeuvrable enemy fighter. Against such an opponent the German pilots' proven tactic was to climb above the enemy, move into a position of advantage, then convert altitude into speed and attack in a dive. Whether or not the attack was successful, the Messerschmitt pilot would pull back into a zoom climb to get above the enemy, where he could assess the situation and decide on his next move.

National pride being what it is, it will come as no surprise that a similar trial carried out at the *Luftwaffe* test centre at Rechlin near Berlin using a captured Spitfire I 'proved' that the Bf 109 was the superior fighter. The Spitfire in that trial had been captured intact during the Dunkirk evacuation. It was fitted with the old two-speed propeller. As a result its climbing performance was inferior to that of the Spitfire used in the Farnborough trials. Also, German pilots were quick to discover that the carburettor float of the Merlin engine ceased to deliver fuel if the pilot pushed down the nose of his aircraft and applied negative 'G', with the result that the engine cut out. The Bf 109 with its fuel injection system did not suffer from this failing.

One German pilot who tried both the Spitfire and the Hurricane during the summer of 1940 was *Maj* Werner Mölders, in June 1940 the top-scoring *Luftwaffe* fighter pilot of the war with 25 aerial victories. His comments are therefore worthy of note:

"It was very interesting to carry out the flight trials at Rechlin with the Spitfire and the Hurricane. Both types are very simple to fly compared with our aircraft and childishly easy to take-off and land. The Hurricane is very good-natured and turns well but its performance is decidedly inferior to that of the Bf 109. It has strong stick forces and is 'lazy' on the ailerons.

"The Spitfire is one class better. It handles well, is light on the controls, faultless in the turn and has a performance approaching that of the Bf 109. As a fighting aircraft, however, it is miserable. A sudden push forward on the stick will cause the motor to cut. And because the propeller has only two pitch settings [take-off and high speed], in a rapidly changing air combat situation the motor is either over-speeding or else is not being used to the full."

Both nations' trials produced results that were valid only up to a point. The British one had been flown at medium altitude turning fight because that was where the Spitfire was the better. The German trial had been flown at high altitude, simulating a high-speed combat because there the Messerschmitt was the better. When the air battle really began, most fighter-versus-fighter combats took place at altitudes between 13,000 and 20,000 ft because that was where the German bombers and their escorts were. And in that height band the performance of the Spitfire I and the Bf 109 E was much closer than either trial had suggested. In the sort of fleeting combat that would become the norm between the opposing fighters, possession of the tactical initiative would count for much more than the relatively minor differences between the two fighter types.

Aces to be: blue section of No 92 Squadron pictured during the Dunkirk evacuation when all three pilots scored their first aerial victories. From left to right they are: Plt Off Bob Holland (later to be credited with 13 victories), Fg Off Robert Stanford-Tuck (29 victories) and Plt Off Alan Wright (10 victories).

A Spitfire of No 72 Squadron displaying the RN code letters introduced in February 1940. Note the 'blinker' in front and to one side of the cockpit to prevent glare from the engine exhaust destroying the pilot's night vision. There was a similar fitting on the starboard side.

Spitfire L1090 was shipped to Canada in May 1940 to fly in mock combat against a USAAF XP-40 at Wright Field, Ohio.

All hailing from Leeds, Bradford and other West Riding cities, these groundcrew were typical of the men who kept No 609 Squadron's 15 Spitfires serviceable throughout the early war years. Whilst the squadron's complement of pre-war auxiliary pilots slowly dwindled in number as the conflict progressed, over 40 'local' groundcrew remained with 609 Squadron well into 1941. Lacking a bullet-proof windscreen and still fitted with a two-speed propeller, this unidentified Spitfire Mk 1 was photographed chocked at Drem during the winter of 1939-40.

4 THE BATTLE OF BRITAIN

Left: This action photograph was taken at Gravesend in late September 1940, and it shows a No 66 Squadron Spitfire coming in to land at the completion of a patrol. In the foreground is R6800, which was regularly flown by the unit's CO, Sqn Ldr Rupert 'Lucky' Leigh. He had the fighter adorned with a rarely seen pre-war rank pennant below the cockpit, as well as an insignia red propeller spinner. Leigh had ordered that the standard black spinner on R6800 be immediately repainted after he was almost shot down in error by a section of Hurricanes. He believed that any potential attacker would be so surprised by the gaudily-marked spinner that he would have a good look at his fighter prior to closing in for the kill! Parked behind R6800 is a Hurricane I of No 501 'County of Gloucester' Sqn, which also operated out of Gravesend at the time, despite technically being based at Kenley.

An armourer at Duxford re-arms a Spitfire of No 19 Squadron during the battle.

THE part Spitfires played during the Battle of Britain has been well documented elsewhere and it is not intended to repeat that coverage in this account. Instead, it will focus on a single day – 18 August 1940 - on which Spitfires participated in some of the heaviest fighting and consider some of the implications.

On the evening before the action, Fighter Command's Spitfire and Hurricane squadrons reported 1,026 aircraft on strength. Of that total roughly two-thirds were Hurricanes and one-third were Spitfires. It is part of the accepted wisdom that the Hurricane was the more robust of the two aircraft and so better able to cope with the rough and tumble of combat than the Spitfire. In truth, there was little to choose between the two fighter types on that score. Of the 347 Spitfires on strength, 276 (79 per cent) were serviceable compared with 549 of the 679 Hurricanes (80 per cent).

On 18 August the *Luftwaffe* planned large-scale raids on three target sets in southern England. The first, scheduled to commence soon after 13.00 hrs, involved a coordinated high and low level attack by 36 Dornier 17s and 12 Junkers 88s of *Kampfgeschwader* 76 on the Fighter Command airfield at Kenley. A few minutes later there would be a high level attack by 60 Heinkel 111s of *Kampfgeschwader* 1 on the nearby airfield at Biggin Hill. The second raid, at 14.30 hrs, involved 109 Junkers Ju 87 dive-bombers drawn from *Sturzkampfgeschwader* 3 and of StG 77. These were to deliver simultaneous attacks on the airfields at Thorney Island, Gosport and Ford and the radar station at Poling.

The third raid, at 17.30 hrs, involved 51 He 111s of KG 53 attacking the airfield at North Weald, followed a few minutes later by an attack by 58 Dorniers of KG 2 on the nearby airfield at Hornchurch. Accompanying each raiding force was a sizeable contingent of Messerschmitt Bf 109 and Bf 110 escorts. In this selection of targets, the *Luftwaffe* was clearly going for Fighter Command's jugular vein. Kenley, Biggin Hill, Hornchurch and North Weald were the four most important sector airfields in No 11 Group. If one or more

of those airfields could be put out of action for any length of time, it would greatly assist the German cause.

Ford was not a Fighter Command airfield but its importance lay in the fact that it housed the Fleet Air Arm torpedo school. Another important unit based there was No 826 Squadron Fleet Air Arm, the first unit to be equipped with the new Fairey Albacore torpedo bomber. Thorney Island was the base for two squadrons of Coastal Command Blenheims. If the invasion of England was launched, both airfields were likely to play an important role. The same went for the radar station at Poling. The reason for the inclusion of Gosport in the target list is unclear: it was the scene of little activity and it operated a few non-operational types.

This account will focus on the early-afternoon series of attacks, which saw the largest ever attack by Ju 87 dive-bombers on Great Britain: 109 *Stukas* escorted by 157 Bf 109s. This force was detected on radar in good time and the RAF fighter controller directed Nos 152, 234 and 602 Squadrons with 34 Spitfires and three more squadrons of 31 Hurricanes into position to intercept. It was a beautiful summer's day, with blue skies and just a few puffs of cloud. Two Hurricane squadrons forced their way through the escorts and caught a *Gruppe* of dive-bombers about to commence their attack on Thorney Island.

The Hurricanes shot down at least three Ju 87s in short order. Then, once the Ju 87s had started their 80-degree attack dives they were relatively safe from fighter attack. With its speed controlled by

its effective underwing dive brakes, the Ju 87 then made a frustrating target. Hurricane pilot Flt Lt Frank Carey of No 43 Squadron during that action, commented: "In the dive they [the Ju 87s] were very difficult to hit because in a fighter one's speed built up so rapidly that one went screaming past him. But he couldn't dive for ever."

After the *Stukas* had released their bombs and pulled out of their dives they withdrew to the south at low altitude in a large untidy gaggle. That gave them the appearance of an ill-disciplined stampede but there was method in this apparent madness. If a fighter closed on an individual dive-bomber from its rear it had only to accelerate and move into a position about 100 yards in front of one of its companions. If the fighter persisted with its attack, it placed the second *Stuka* in a perfect position to engage the fighter from behind at short range using its two forward-firing machine guns.

The 25-mile strip of coastline between Bognor and Gosport now became a mass of some 300 aircraft, twisting and turning to bring guns to bear or to avoid guns being brought to bear. Flt Lt Derek Boitel-Gill ordered the 11 Spitfires of No 152 Squadron to move into line astern and then led them into the melee. He picked out a

Above and left: Spitfires of No 609 Squadron photographed early in the battle, probably when the unit was operating from Warmwell as part of No 10 Group.

Background image: The UK population often had a grandstand seat during the hot summer of 1940 – watching the exhaust contrails as the RAF and Luftwaffe often fought it out at very high altitudes over the south-east of England. This often silent but deadly aerial ballet was occasionally punctuated by the distant rattle of gunfire and screaming engines.

Armourers feverishly re-arm a Spitfire between sorties during the battle. The eight-gun Spitfire (and Hurricane) took a lot of effort, as cleaning the eight guns, fitting eight 300-round belts of ammunition and checking the compressed air created quite a workload. Experienced ground-crews could do this in as little as ten minutes.

Now fully re-armed with the engine ticking over (not the same Spitfire as above) a ground crewman makes last checks with the pilot, before jumping down and removing the wheel chocks. Note the difference in underwing roundel sizes on both these Spitfires and the resealed gun ports with canvas patches.

out a small bunch of dive-bombers heading south, aimed a 4-second burst into one of them and saw it crash into the sea. He then shifted his attack to another *Stuka* but then had to break away when Messerschmitts swept in to protect their charges.

The twelve Spitfires of No 602 Squadron caught up with the *Stukas* of II./StG 77 just after they left the coast near Middleton-on-Sea. Flt Lt Dunlop Urie in the lead fired bursts at five dive-bombers in turn before he ran out of ammunition. Sgt Basil Whall singled out one Ju 87 and made four deliberate attacks before it curved back towards the coast and force-landed near Rustington. Whall then sped out to sea for another go at the dive-bombers and engaged one from 50 yards. The fighter's rounds raked the *Stuka*, which caught fire and crashed into the sea. In the course of these attacks, however, Whall appears to have fallen foul of the Germans' 'gaggle trap' tactic. His Spitfire took numerous hits and, his engine losing power, he made a forced landing on the beach near Middleton-on-Sea.

As the melee moved south, Plt Off Bob Doe of No 234 Squadron noticed that a few Messerschmitts had stayed behind and were shooting up barrage balloons over Portsmouth. Doe picked one of the enemy fighters and accelerated after it. His opponent saw him

A pair of No 616 Sqn Spitfire Is glide in over the perimeter at Kirton-in-Lindsey after completing yet another training flight in mid-September 1940. A standard landing during this time would see the pilot fly a curved approach so as to enable him to keep the airfield in sight at all times. The canopy hood was locked open and the side door left ajar in the half-cocked position so as to avoid the hood slamming shut in a mishap. The pilot then checked the brake pressure and extended the undercarriage, the latter only being dropped at speeds below 160 mph – two green lights and indicator bars out told the pilot that the wheels were down and locked. A rich engine mixture was selected, the propeller pitch lever moved to fully fine and the flaps deployed (only below 140 mph). With all this completed, the pilot aimed to 'fly over the hedge' at 85 mph indicated and then ease back on the stick to keep the Spitfire off the grass until its speed was down to 64 mph. The fighter would then gently stall onto the runway. Flown for the first time on the last day of August 1940, X4330 'QJ-G' was delivered to No 616 Sqn exactly a week later, and it served with the unit into 1941.

Line-up of Spitfires at the Flying Legends Air Show at Duxford in July 2008. At the time of writing the newly-overhauled aircraft in the foreground, Mk 1, AR213, is the only example of an airworthy Mk 1 Spitfire. It is displayed in the markings when it was flown by James Harry 'Ginger' Lacey, a flight instructor of No 57 OTU (Operational Training Unit) in August 1941. Lacey was one of the most successful fighter pilots in the RAF – by November 1940 he had 23 claims (18 made during the Battle of Britain).

Sgt Basil Whall flew with No 602 Squadron and was credited with six victories and two shared during the battle. He was killed in action on 7 October 1940.

Junkers Ju 87 dive-bomber shot down by Basil Whall on 18 August 1940.

Below: Plt Off Robert Doe of No 234 Squadron, left, was credited with the destruction of a Bf 109 on 18 August. His total score while flying Spitfires was 11 enemy aircraft destroyed and two shared destroyed. In September 1940 he transferred to a Hurricane squadron and shot down three more enemy aircraft. He survived the war.

coming, opened the throttle and headed for home. Doe recalled:

"He saw me, put down his nose and went dead straight for France. He did not do any turns at all. He went down to about 100 ft and just kept on going with me gaining on him very slowly."

After a long chase and a few experimental bursts, Doe found his opponent's range and saw his rounds strike home. The Messerschmitt began to lose speed, its canopy flew away, then the pilot baled out. Short of fuel, Doe headed for home without waiting to observe his victim's fate. The main action lasted about 6 minutes from the time the leading dive-bombers crossed the coast until the last of them left the area. At the same time the RAF fighters, having exhausted their ammunition or run short of fuel, broke off their attacks and headed for home. Dunlop Urie was nearing his base at Westhampnett when he noticed another fighter closing on him. He thought it looked like a Spitfire but he was mistaken. The next thing he knew was a series of loud bangs as cannon shells detonated on his rear fuselage. Splinters from the exploding rounds gouged into his legs. Urie managed to avoid further attacks and brought his damaged fighter back to his base. But the Spitfire's back was broken and was pronounced damaged beyond repair.

Supermarine Spitfire Mk I, QV-K, P9386, flown by Squadron Leader Brian Lane, CO of 19 Squadron, Duxford, September 1940
Camouflaged in dark earth, dark green over Duck Egg Green with medium Sea Grey codes. Previous information states the spinner was yellow, but this is speculative.

Brian Lane was credited with four aerial victories during the battle, plus one before and one after, to take his total score to six. He was killed in action in December 1942.

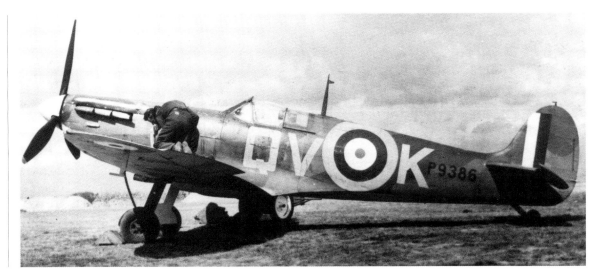

Spitfire deployment on 17 August 1940

Spitfire units on the afternoon of 17 August 1940, early in the Battle of Britain. The first figure indicates the number of aircraft serviceable, while that in brackets shows aircraft unserviceable.

No 10 Group, HQ Box, Wiltshire

Middle Wallop Sector			
No 152 Squadron	13	(2)	Warmwell
No 609 Squadron	13	(5)	Middle Wallop
No 234 Squadron	16	(1)	Middle Wallop
Filton Sector			
No 92 Squadron	16	(2)	Pembrey
Group Total	**58**	**(10)**	

No 11 Group, HQ Uxbridge, Middlesex

Kenley Hill Sector			
No 64 Squadron	12	(5)	Kenley
Biggin Hill			
No 610 Squadron	19	(1)	Biggin Hill
Hornchurch Sector			
No 54 Squadron	14	(5)	Hornchurch
No 266 Squadron	12	(7)	Hornchurch
No 65 Squadron	13	(7)	Rochford
Tangmere Sector			
No 602 Squadron	18	(3)	Westhampnett
Group Total	**88**	**(28)**	

No 12 Group, HQ Watnall, Nottinghamshire

Duxford Sector			
No 19 Squadron	15	(4)	Duxford
Coltishall Sector			
No 66 Squadron	15	(3)	Coltishall
Wittering Sector			
No 74 Squadron	17	(5)	Wittering
Digby Sector			
No 611 Squadron	24	(3)	Digby
Kirton-in-Lindsey Sector			
No 222 Squadron	16	(3)	Kirton-in-Lindsey
Church Fenton Sector			
No 616 Squadron	13	(4)	
Group Total	**100**	**(22)**	

No 13 Group, HQ Newcastle, Northumberland

Catterick Sector			
No 41 Squadron	16	(2)	Catterick
Acklington Sector			
No 72 Squadron	14	(4)	Acklington
Turnhouse Sector			
No 603 Squadron	14	(8)	Turnhouse
Group Total	**44**	**(14)**	

Flt Lt Derek Boitel-Gill served as a flight commander with No 152 Squadron. During the battle he was credited with eight aerial victories, plus one shared. He was killed in a flying accident in September 1941.

Sqn Ldr Donald Macdonnell commanded No 64 Squadron during the battle when his total score was nine aerial victories and one shared. He was shot down and taken prisoner in March 1941.

During this action 17 dive-bombers had been destroyed or damaged beyond repair and seven more returned with battle damage. Eight of the escorting Messerschmitts were also shot down. In this successful engagement RAF Fighter Command's losses amounted to three fighters destroyed or damaged beyond repair, and eight more damaged.

The signature of any Ju 87 attack was the extreme accuracy of the bombing. Ford airfield was hit hardest. Huge fires destroyed two Albacores, five Swordfish and five obsolescent Blackburn Shark torpedo bombers. A further 15 Sharks were damaged. At Thorney Island a Blenheim was destroyed and a Wellington damaged. At Gosport nine non-operational aircraft were destroyed or damaged.

The *Luftwaffe* also launched heavy attacks on the important Fighter Command sector stations at Kenley, Biggin Hill, Hornchurch and North Weald. How successful were they? Although Kenley was the hardest hit, it was out of action for only a few hours. After significant craters had been filled in and rolled flat, the airfield was operating almost normally by the following day. Biggin Hill was also hit hard but the cratering of its grass surface was not serious enough to prevent fighter operations. Neither Hornchurch nor North Weald was hit that day. In the late afternoon a blanket of cloud drifted over these airfields, forcing the raiders to abandon

"We found about 30 Ju 87s making for France"

Plt Off Eric Marrs took part in the action against the dive-bombers off the coast of Sussex on 18 August. Afterwards he wrote to his father:

"There was a large-scale raid on Southampton [sic] and Gosport consisting of Ju 87s escorted by Me 109s. We arrived on the scene just as the 87s had finished dropping bombs. There were other squadrons already there and we have since learnt that one of them took on the fighter escort. We were therefore lucky and when we arrived we found about 30 Ju 87s making for France. We met them just off the east end of the Isle of Wight. We dived after them and they went down to about 100 ft above the water. Then followed a running chase out to sea. The evasive action they took was to throttle back and do steep turns to right and left so that we would not be able to follow them and would overshoot. There were, however, so many of them that if one was shaken off the tail of one there was always another to sit on. I fired at about six and shot down one. It caught fire in the port wing petrol tank and then went into the sea about 300 yards farther on.

"When I had finished my ammunition I turned away and found an Me 109 sitting on my tail. As I turned it fired a burst in front of me. I could see the tracer and I seemed to fly right through it. I was not hit, however, and ran for home as it was senseless staying without ammunition. I was not followed and two other chaps shot down that 109 soon after."

Lucky escape for Plt Off Alan Wright of No 92 Squadron. During a combat with Messerschmitt Bf 109s on 9 September an enemy round fired from behind passed through his Perspex canopy, bounced off the inside of the toughened glass windscreen and smashed his reflector gun sight. Wright was fortunate to escape without injury.

their primary targets and instead bomb targets of opportunity on the way home.

During the action as a whole on 18 August, the *Luftwaffe* lost 69 aircraft destroyed or damaged beyond repair, while RAF Fighter Command lost 31 fighters on the same basis with seven more destroyed on the ground. A further 29 aircraft, none of them fighters, were destroyed on the ground during the attacks on Gosport, Thorney Island and Ford. Examination of these statistics reveals some interesting points. In the various actions, Spitfires and Hurricanes flew 320 sorties and achieved victories in direct proportion to the number taking part in each engagement. Where there was a marked difference between the two fighter types was in their ability to survive in combat. On 18 August Fighter Command lost 30 single-seat fighters in air combat. Of these, 25 were Hurricanes (8.4 per cent of those committed) and five were Spitfires (4.5 per cent of those committed). This indicated that a Hurricane engaging the enemy was only about half as likely to survive the encounter as a Spitfire. With its significantly better performance, the Spitfire was far less likely to be 'bounced' from above by enemy fighters and that greatly increased its chance of survival. On other hard-fought days in the battle the Spitfire would demonstrate a significant edge in survivability, though rarely was it as great as on 18 August.

The Junkers Ju 87 was the most effective precision attack weapon available to the *Luftwaffe* and the force could not afford another day with a 15 per cent loss rate. These aircraft had to be conserved to support the planned invasion of Britain and the type played little further part in the battle.

The attacks on the Fighter Command airfields continued for another three weeks although without noteworthy success. No matter how often they came under attack the Fighter Sector airfields were always repaired and back in full or nearly full use by the following day.

Aside from the three 'Yanks' who served with No 609 Squadron during the battle, the Canadians also had a presence in the 'West Riding' squadron in the form of Plt Off Keith Ogilvie. A future ace, the Ottawan arrived at the unit on 20 August, and served in the front line until shot down and captured on 4 July 1941. He subsequently took part in the Great Escape in March 1944, but was recaptured after two days on the run. Ogilvie is seen here smoking his pipe and enjoying a joke with 'Red' Tobin whilst at readiness in front of No 609 Sqn's Watch Office at Middle Wallop – both pilots were assigned to 'A' Flight, and regularly flew together. Note the American's preference for flying boots (into which he has tucked a map) and full service dress.

Right: The high rate of sorties flown during the battle imposed severe strains on airmen on both sides. This photograph depicts pilots of No 65 Squadron at `30 minutes available' readiness at Gravesend.

Fg Off Leonard Haines flew with No 19 Squadron during the battle in which he was credited with six aerial victories, plus two shared. He had scored one more before the battle and another plus two shared afterwards. He was killed in a flying accident in April 1941.

This Spitfire I (N3024 'PR-H') of 609 Squadron was lost near Weymouth on 14 August whilst being flown by Flg Off Henry 'Mac' Goodwin. Scrambled in the wake of the devastating surprise raid on Middle Wallop by Ju 88s of 1./LG 1, Goodwin (who had claimed three kills in the previous two days) headed south and simply disappeared. Flying alone, he was almost certainly 'bounced' by enemy fighters, for a Spitfire was seen to crash into the sea off Boscombe Pier in Dorset a short while later. The pilot succeeded in baling out, but no trace of him could be found. Ten days later 'Mac' Goodwin's body was washed ashore on the Isle of Wight. This photograph shows a mission-ready N3024 and its groundcrew at Middle Wallop in early August. Parked behind 'PR-H' is Spitfire I L1096 'PR-G', which survived its long spell with No 609 Sqn, and was later passed on to the Fleet Air Arm.

S HORTLY before the outbreak of war Flg Off Maurice 'Shorty' Longbottom wrote a memorandum on the future of strategic aerial reconnaissance in the Royal Air Force. In the paper he stressed the need to avoid enemy fighter and AA defences wherever possible. He wrote: "The best method of doing this appears to be the use of a single small machine, relying solely on its speed, climb and ceiling to avoid detection."

In Longbottom's view, an ideal aircraft for the long-range reconnaissance role was a modified Spitfire. He argued that removing the guns and ammunition boxes, the radio and other items of equipment not required for the reconnaissance role, would shave 450 lbs off the weight of the Spitfire. Moreover, the Spitfire could get airborne even if it was overloaded by as much as 480 lbs. So there was 930 lbs of lifting capacity available for the carriage of cameras and extra fuel tankage.

The proposal to employ an unarmed high-speed, high-flying single-seater aircraft for this important role was a radical departure from accepted military thinking. At that time the Bristol Blenheim was the RAF's sole long-range reconnaissance type. It retained its defensive armament, ostensibly so it could fight its way through to its target and back again. Yet those guns and the gunner imposed a substantial performance penalty, which brought the aircraft within reach of the very defences it needed to avoid if it was to carry out its mission effectively.

Initially Longbottom's paper brought little response. The RAF was desperately short of modern fighters and the entire production of Spitfires was allocated to Fighter Command for the defence of the home islands. The breakthrough for his ideas came in the late autumn of 1939 after the loss of several Blenheims flying daylight photographic reconnaissance missions over Germany. Moreover, due to the harassment from the defences, the surviving

Blenheims often returned without any photographs of intelligence value.

After a brief period of discussion, Air Chief Marshal Dowding agreed to part with two of his precious Spitfires for reconnaissance duties. At Heston airfield north of London, a secret unit commanded by Wg Cdr Sidney Cotton was formed to convert the Spitfires for their new role. The unit was designated 'The Heston Flight' and, appropriately, one of the first officers posted in was 'Shorty' Longbottom.

The first priority was to modify a Spitfire and take photographs of enemy territory to show up any unforeseen flaws in Longbottom's proposals. A camera was fitted in each wing fixed to look vertically downwards. The aircraft was then 'cleaned up' to give the last ounce of speed: the empty gun ports were sealed with metal plates and all external joints were filled with plaster of Paris and rubbed down to

Photographic reconnaissance Spitfire PR 1B captured by German troops at Champagne airfield near Reims after they had overrun the area in June 1940.

The Spitfire PR 1C reconnaissance variant carried its vertically-mounted cameras in a blister under the starboard wing, seen here with the door open. Under the port wing was another blister housing a 30-gal fuel tank.

The Spitfire PR ID had an integral fuel tank running along the leading edge of each wing, each with a capacity of 61.5 gal. This gave rise to the unusual sight of a Spitfire being refuelled at a filler near the wing tip.

Only one Spitfire Type PR1E was built. This variant carried an oblique camera under each wing, looking outwards at right angles to the direction of flight.

give a smooth external finish. Earlier, Cotton had noticed that a distant aircraft seen from below usually appeared as a dark silhouette against the light sky background. So he ordered the Spitfire to be painted in a light shade of pale green to make it less conspicuous from below.

In the autumn of 1939 Cotton's unit was renamed 'No 2 Camouflage Unit' to explain the odd colouring of its aircraft. Spitfire N3071 flew to Seclin near Lille in northern France to prepare for operations. On 18 November Longbottom, now a flight lieutenant,

"It was like a fox hunt."

Plt Off Gordon Green joined the Photographic Reconnaissance Unit at Heston in December 1940 and began flying Spitfires on operations from Benson in the following February. He commented:

"A big worry over enemy territory was that one might start leaving a condensation trail without knowing it, thus pointing out one's position to the enemy. To avoid that we had small mirrors fitted in the blisters on each side of the canopy, so that one could see the trail as soon as it started to form behind. When that happened one could either climb or descend until the trail ceased. If possible, we liked to climb above the trail's layer. That was because any fighter trying to intercept us had first to climb through the trail's layer, allowing us to see him in good time.

"Whenever it was possible to photograph a target, flak could engage us: if we could see [the target] they could see to open up at us. But throughout my time as a reconnaissance pilot my luck held. I never once saw an enemy fighter, nor was my aircraft ever hit by flak. Indeed, only once during the time we were flying those missions over Brest did one of our aircraft come back with any damage and that was only minor. It was all rather like a fox hunt – either the fox got away unscathed or else it was caught and killed. There was rarely anything in between.'

took off to conduct the first Spitfire reconnaissance mission. The target was the German city of Aachen and nearby fortifications. But flying alone at 33,000 ft, navigation proved more difficult than Longbottom had anticipated. As a result, he returned to Seclin with a line of photographs depicting the Belgian side of the frontier south of Aachen. The reason for the failure, incorrect alignment before starting a photo run, was quickly understood and four days later Longbottom successfully photographed the Belgian-German border east of Liege.

During the next six weeks, cloud cover prevented high-altitude photography of northern Germany. But at the end of December the weather cleared and the modified Spitfires, two of which were now available, resumed operations. In short order they photographed Aachen, Cologne, Kaiserslautern, Wiesbaden, Mainz and a large strip

cloud cover. Cotton's unit pioneered low altitude oblique photography, using a fixed camera looking sideways at 90 deg to the line of flight. The oblique camera proved its value during an early mission in July 1940. Flg Off Alistair Taylor arrived at the French coast to find his target, Boulogne harbour, with a 700 ft cloud base in heavy rain. He ran past the port of Boulogne at 300 ft and photographed the harbour without alerting the defences. Henceforth the low-altitude photography of small targets, nicknamed 'dicing' because of the risks involved, became an important role for reconnaissance Spitfires.

Far left: The Spitfire PR 1G retained its armament of eight machine guns for defence. It was employed on low altitude 'dicing' missions and on photographing targets below cloud. These aircraft were often painted a shade of pink so pale it was almost off-white – the colour of the bottom of cloud observed on an overcast day.

of the Ruhr industrial area. Significantly, this was done without a single loss or, except on one occasion, any significant interference from the German defences.

Although Longbottom's basic concept had been proved beyond doubt, there was considerable scope for building on it. Even after the film prints were blown up as large as the grain of the film would allow, pictures taken from 33,000 ft with the 5 in focal length cameras produced pictures of a small scale. Roads, railways, villages and major fortifications could be picked out but anything smaller was likely to be missed. The answer was to fit cameras with longer telephoto lenses to give a better definition of ground features. Also the reconnaissance Spitfires needed additional fuel tanks, to increase their radius of action.

During 1940 progressive increases in the Spitfires' fuel tankage enabled the aircraft to penetrate deeper and deeper into enemy territory. In February the limit from bases in England was Wilhelmshaven; in April it was Kiel and in October Stettin on the Baltic (now Szczecin in Poland). In November a Spitfire photographed Marseilles in the south of France. Better cameras for high altitude work also appeared, first with 8 in, then 14 in, 20 in and later 36 in telephoto lenses.

Vertical photography from high altitude was the best way to cover large areas of ground, or cities on clear days. But another technique was needed to photograph small targets or from a point beneath

Dramatic low altitude oblique shot of a Giant Wuerzburg fighter control radar on the Dutch island of Walcheren. As the Spitfire swept past the radar, one of the operators stood watching it from beside the entry ladder. The man would serve as a human yardstick when RAF photo interpreters came to analyse the picture and gauge the size of the installation.

Left: Flt Lt Gordon Hughes pictured with a PR 1G. The window for the port-facing oblique camera is immediately to the left of the fuselage roundel.

As the unit became more experienced, its aircraft were repainted in new and more effective colours depending on their specialised role. Those fitted with long focal length vertical cameras were painted in medium blue to make them as inconspicuous as possible at high altitude, while those with oblique cameras for low-altitude 'dicing' missions were painted in a pale shade of pink, barely off-white, to make them difficult to see from below against a cloud background. This scheme would, of course, make them highly conspicuous when seen from above if there was no cloud cover.

Throughout 1940 the Spitfire reconnaissance force was continually being reorganised. In January No 2 Camouflage Unit was renamed the Photographic Development Unit (PDU) and in July it was renamed the Photographic Reconnaissance Unit (PRU). By then it operated 12 reconnaissance Spitfires with various modification states, now commanded by Wg Cdr Geoffrey Tuttle who had replaced Cotton the previous month.

Throughout the dark days of 1940 and 1941 the PRU Spitfires kept a daily watch on the ports in France, Holland and Belgium where barges and other ships were assembling for the threatened invasion of England. The photo interpreters kept a running tally of the ships and barges present at each port. And when the invasion was 'postponed' after the failure of the *Luftwaffe* to defeat the RAF during the Battle of Britain, the PRU Spitfires' photographs recorded the drift of barges away from invasion ports.

Although one major danger had receded, there were plenty of others to occupy the PRU Spitfires. In the spring of 1941 there was a requirement for them to photograph Brest harbour three times each day to check that the battle cruisers *Scharnhorst* and *Gneisenau* were still in port. If these powerful warships emerged for a destructive foray into the Atlantic the Admiralty would need to revise its dispositions immediately to protect the all-important Allied convoys. These operations were considered so important that Spitfires set out in pairs to give the greatest chance of securing the required photographs. A blue-painted aircraft flew over the port at high altitude if there was no cloud cover. If there was a blanket of cloud, a pink aircraft would run in over the port at low altitude to take oblique photographs.

In November the unit was redesignated yet again and became No 1 Photographic Reconnaissance Unit to distinguish it from another PRU being formed in the Mediterranean theatre. And in December it left Heston for the larger airfield at Benson near Oxford which offered much better facilities. By the summer of 1942 No 1 PRU had a strength of 53 Spitfires as well as 12 Mosquitoes modified for reconnaissance operations. These aircraft ranged far and wide over Germany and occupied Europe and had the speed and altitude performance to do so without incurring undue risk. The pioneering days were over and this type of reconnaissance was an accepted and important part of the Royal Air Force's capability. Longbottom's far-sighted concept had been developed to its logical conclusion.

Left: Interior of the huge Spitfire production facility at Castle Bromwich near Birmingham built by Morris Motors under contract to the British government. During the war the plant produced some 12,000 Spitfires, more than half of the total. At its peak it was turning out 320 Spitfires per month.

A large part of the workforce at Castle Bromwich comprised women, some of whom are pictured here gluing 'Linatex' self-sealing rubber coverings to Spitfire fuel tanks.

O N 26 September 1940 a force of 59 Heinkel 111s of *Kampfgeschwader* 55 delivered devastating attacks on the two large Supermarine factories at Woolston and Itchen. The raiders wrecked the main factory buildings at both sites, striking a severe blow at Spitfire production.

The next day Lord Beaverbrook, Winston Churchill's energetic Minister of Aircraft Production, visited Southampton to gauge the extent of the damage. The attacks highlighted the extreme vulnerability of the main Supermarine factories located near the south coast. Both factories were damaged beyond economical repair and Beaverbrook ordered that the two factories be abandoned.

Henceforth their production of Spitfires was to be dispersed into several much smaller units situated in towns and cities spread over a large area. Fortunately, most Spitfire production jigs and machine tools at Woolston and Itchen had survived the attacks and been removed to places of safety. Also, the hangars at Eastleigh airfield, used for Spitfire final assembly, had not come under attack.

Establishing the dispersed production facilities involved an immense amount of work. Supermarine executives toured Southampton, Winchester, Salisbury, Trowbridge, Reading and Newbury and their surrounding areas searching for any buildings that could be pressed into use for aircraft production. Motor repair garages, bus stations and large laundries were the obvious choices. A policeman accompanied each Supermarine executive with a letter of introduction from the local chief constable requesting cooperation but giving no reason for the visit. When a building was considered suitable for the dispersed production scheme, the usually less-than-delighted owner received official papers to requisition the building. As each new site was acquired, the Spitfire production jigs and machine tools were brought in and set up. By the end of October 1940, 35 separate premises had been requisitioned for the dispersal programme and production had already begun at 16 of them.

Meanwhile, in the summer of 1940, large-scale production of Spitfires had also begun at the purpose-built factory at Castle Bromwich near Birmingham. Never again would Spitfire production be as vulnerable to air attack as it had been in September 1940.

Left: Installing a Merlin 46 engine into a Spitfire V. This engine developed 1,515 hp (1,130 kW) at 3,000 rpm at 11,000 ft (3,353 m); and was used in the Spitfire Mk V, PR Mk IV and PR Mk VII, Seafire Ib and IIc.

Assembling an instrument panel for a Spitfire.

Alex Henshaw, chief test pilot at Castle Bromwich, second from the right, personally test flew no fewer than 2,360 Spitfires, about one in ten of those built.

Above and opposite page: As well as the huge factory at Castle Bromwich, small-scale production of Spitfires and components took place at several sites across the south of England. Vincent's garage at Reading was one such and produced Spitfire fuselages.

A newly-built Spitfire V takes off for its works test flight. The aircraft has a dust filter fitted beneath its nose and is probably destined for the Middle East.

7 RAF FIGHTER COMMAND TAKES THE OFFENSIVE

EARLY in 1941 RAF Fighter Command opened a campaign of offensive air operations over occupied Europe. With the bulk of the *Luftwaffe* redeploying into airfields in East Prussia, Poland and Rumania for the attack on the Soviet Union, there was a marked reduction in air activity against Britain. When the attack on the Soviet Union opened, in June 1941, there was a political imperative for Britain to support her new ally and tie down in the west as many *Luftwaffe* units as possible.

The main types of offensive operation over occupied Europe undertaken by RAF Fighter Command were code-named as follows:

Circus: Attack by a small force of bombers with powerful fighter escort, intended to lure enemy fighters into the air so they could be engaged by RAF fighters. The primary objectives were the destruction of enemy fighters and protection of the bombers

Ramrod: Attack by bombers (or fighter-bombers) escorted by fighters; the primary object was the destruction of the target and the fighters' primary role was to protect the bombers

Rhubarb: Small-scale attack by fighters using cloud cover and surprise with the object of destroying enemy aircraft in the air and/or striking at ground targets

Roadstead: Attack on enemy ships at sea by bombers (or fighter/bombers) escorted by fighters

Rodeo: Fighter sweep over enemy territory with no bombers.

Coincident with the revision of RAF operational policy, the second major variant of the Spitfire entered production. This was the Mk V powered by the new Merlin 45 engine. This generated an extra 500 hp, which increased the fighter's maximum speed to 371 mph, giving it near parity with the Messerschmitt Bf 109 F, the latest variant of the German fighter then entering *Luftwaffe* service in quantity.

During 1941 the production of Spitfire Vs greatly exceeded losses, allowing a rapid expansion in the number of squadrons equipped

Left: Sqn Ldr James Rankin, CO of No 92 Squadron, pictured in the summer of 1941 when his score stood at 10 enemy aircraft destroyed. He ended the war credited with 17 aircraft destroyed and five shared victories.

Polish fighter pilots of 303 Squadron 'scramble' in this staged photograph for the camera sometime in 1941. The Spitfire in the background has Rotol propellor blades and fishtail exhausts, making it most likely a Mk. Vb.

with the type. It quickly replaced the Hurricane in home defence fighter units as well as earlier Spitfires. During the Battle of Britain there had been 19 squadrons operating Spitfires; by September 1941 there were 27. And by the end of 1941 Fighter Command possessed 46 squadrons equipped with Spitfires.

Although the performance of the Spitfire V was significantly better than that of earlier variants, by the autumn of 1941 even it was overtaken by the latest product of the German aircraft industry. For a new and even more effective fighter had just entered service in the

Luftwaffe: the Focke-Wulf Fw 190. When it was encountered in action it posed a severe threat to Fighter Command's activities (see page 62-63). Fortunately for the RAF, however, the *Luftwaffe* was heavily committed to supporting the campaign against the Soviet Union. The size of the fighter force retained in the west, equipped mainly with Fw 190s, remained relatively small at around 200 aircraft.

Clip-winged Spitfire V of No 401 (Canadian) Squadron. Below 10,000 ft the modification gave improved acceleration, a higher diving speed and a greater rate of roll. Note the 'shark's mouth' on the Tiger Moth behind.

Hero worship: Air Training Corps cadets hang on every word as Sgt Don Kingaby of No 92 Squadron describes what it is like to fly the Spitfire in combat. By the end of the war Kingaby's score stood at 21 enemy aircraft destroyed and two shared victories.

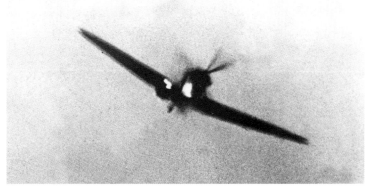

Spitfire in trouble: a still from a combat film taken by Luftwaffe fighter ace Maj Gerhard Schoepfel of Jagdgeschwader 26, showing cannon shells detonating against the fuselage of a Spitfire.

SPITFIRE VB VERSUS FOCKE-WULF FW 190 A-3

In July 1942 a Spitfire V was flown in a comparative trial against a captured Focke-Wulf 190. During the previous 10 months RAF pilots became aware that they faced a formidable foe. But the trials revealed just how formidable, as the following excerpts from the official RAF report show.

Speed: The Fw 190 was compared with a Spitfire VB from an operational squadron for speed and all-round manoeuvrability at heights up to 25,000 ft. The Fw 190 was superior in speed at all heights and the approximate differences were that at:

- 2,000 ft the Fw 190 was 25-30 mph faster than the Spitfire VB
- 3,000 ft it was 30-35 mph faster
- 5,000 ft it was 25 mph faster
- 9,000 ft it was 25-30 mph faster
- 15,000 ft it was 20 mph faster
- 18,000 ft it was 20 mph faster
- 21,000 ft it was 20-25 mph faster.

Climb: The Fw 190's climb was superior to that of the Spitfire VB at all heights. The best speeds for climbing were approximately the same but the angle of the Fw 190 was considerably steeper. Under maximum continuous climbing conditions the climb rate of the Fw 190 was about 450 ft/min better up to 25,000 ft.

Dive: Comparative dives between the two aircraft showed that the Fw 190 could leave the Spitfire with ease, particularly during the initial stages.

Manoeuvrability: The Fw 190's manoeuvrability was better than that of the Spitfire VB except in turning circles when the Spitfire could quite easily out-turn it. The Fw 190 had better acceleration under all conditions of flight and this was obviously most useful during combat. When the Fw 190 was in a turn and attacked by the Spitfire, the superior rate of roll enabled it to flick into a diving turn in the opposite direction. The Spitfire pilot would have great difficulty in following this manoeuvre even when prepared for it and was seldom able to allow the correct deflection. A dive from this manoeuvre enabled the Fw 190 to draw away from the Spitfire, which was then forced to break off the attack.

The trials showed that in areas where enemy fighters might be encountered, it was important for the Spitfire VB to cruise at high speed. Then, in addition to lessening the chances of being 'bounced', it would have a better chance of catching the Fw 190, particularly if it had the advantage of surprise.

The Spitfire V bore the brunt of the RAF offensive over occupied Europe in 1941 and until the autumn of 1942, and suffered serious losses at the hands of the defending Focke-Wulf Fw 190 units.

Fw 190 A-3, W.Nr. 5313, on the airfield at Pembrey in South Wales after its pilot, Oblt Armin Faber, the Gruppenadjutant of III./JG 2, landed due to a navigational error after combat with a Spitfire of 310 Squadron on 23 June 1942. This was the first intact Fw 190 that had fallen into Allied hands and was the basis of the first official trials against the Spitfire V, which caused much concern in RAF Fighter Command.

Below: Faber's Fw 190 was repainted in RAF markings, allocated the serial number MP499 and evaluated at Farnborough. It was later sent for evaluation trials at the Air Fighting Development Unit at Duxford. Armin Faber himself was later transferred to a PoW camp in Canada from where, after two failed escape attempts, he was repatriated on grounds of ill health in the closing months of the war.

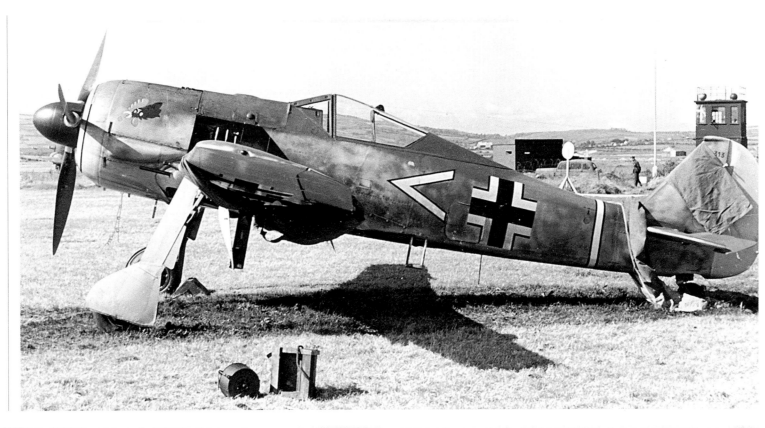

Armin Faber's Fw 190 was flown 29 times by the Royal Air Force between 3 July 1942 and 29 January 1943, for demonstrations and comparison with its British fighter contemporaries. This important aircraft met an undignified end on 18 September 1943, when it was struck off charge after 12 hours of firing trials and destructive testing.

UNTIL March 1942 the entire Spitfire fighter force had been held back for the defence of Britain. Yet, following the expansion of the force, there were Spitfires to spare for other theatres of war. Heading the priority list for such a deployment was the Mediterranean area and in particular Malta.

Britain's strategy in that area hinged on the island's continued use as a base for the bombers and submarines attacking convoys carrying supplies to the Axis forces in North Africa. Yet the besieged island was taking a fearful pounding from German and Italian bombers and its continued survival was in question. Malta's fighter force had declined to about 20 serviceable Hurricanes, which were outclassed by the Messerschmitt Bf 109 Fs opposing them.

Malta urgently needed a force of Spitfires to beef up its air defences and enable it to survive the onslaught. But getting fighters to the island was no simple matter. The Hurricanes already there had been fitted with external ferry tanks. They were transported halfway by aircraft carrier and then launched to fly the rest of the way to the island. Each such operation required a major fleet action, however, and meant sending an invaluable aircraft carrier into a high-risk area. Typically, the carrier required an escort comprising another carrier, a battleship, a cruiser and nine destroyers. The journey from the fly-off point to Malta was about 660 miles, roughly the same as London to Prague. If Hurricanes could reach the island by that method, so could Spitfires. But they first had to be modified for this purpose.

The Supermarine company received a top priority order to prepare a batch of Spitfires for the next re-supply operation, code-named *Spotter*. Engineers hastily designed and built a number of 90 gal drop tanks to fit on attachment points under the Spitfire's fuselage. The fighter's fuel system was also revised to enable it to feed fuel from the drop tank to the engine. Several other modifications were necessary if the Spitfire was to operate successfully in the dusty conditions of the Middle East. One of the biggest problems was caused by dust sucked into the carburettor air intake and entering the engine where it caused excessive wear and a drastic reduction in engine life. To prevent this, a filter unit for the carburettor air intake was mounted in a beard-like fairing under the fighter's nose.

The first delivery of Spitfires to Malta took place on 7 March 1942 when 15 fighters took off from HMS *Eagle* and flew to the island. Before the end of the month the carrier made two further delivery runs, bringing the number of Spitfires flown to the island to 31. They arrived in the nick of time as the *Luftwaffe* had stepped up its attacks on the island as a prelude to the planned invasion. But there were firm limits to what a delivery in dribs and drabs could achieve in this difficult scenario. Heavily outnumbered, the Spitfires were pitch-forked into a desperate battle for survival and the small March delivery of fighters was soon reduced almost to nothing.

It was essential to deliver a more substantial force of Spitfires to the island and Prime Minister Winston Churchill turned to President Roosevelt for help. In a personal telegram he requested that one of the US Navy's big fleet carriers be used to deliver a much larger batch of fighters to Malta. The US president acceded to the request and on 12 April USS *Wasp* put into King George V Dock, Glasgow, and began embarking 47 Spitfires. At first light on 20 April *Wasp* reached the flying-off point and launched the fighters. All except one reached Malta. Yet, such was the ferocity of the air fighting over the island at this time, that within a few days a large proportion of the precious Spitfires had been destroyed in the air or on the ground.

Again the Prime Minister requested a Spitfire delivery operation and again the President agreed. Operation *Bowery*, on 9 May 1942, was the largest such delivery. *Wasp* launched another 47 Spitfires, while the accompanying HMS *Eagle* flew off a further 17. Of the 64 fighters 60 reached Malta. With the survivors of the earlier deliveries,

Spitfire V fitted with four 20 mm cannon arrives by crane on the flight deck of the aircraft carrier USS *Wasp* docked at Glasgow in April 1942. The fighter's wing tips have been removed and stowed in the open cockpit to allow the aircraft to be transported by road from nearby Abbotsinch airfield to the port.

Right: The flight deck of the USS *Wasp* pictured during the late afternoon of 19 April when the carrier prepares to fly off her brood of Spitfires early the following morning. Ranged in front and to the left of the Spitfires are the carrier's own Wildcat fighters, which would take off first to cover the operation.

plus damaged ones repaired and returned to service, there were sufficient Spitfires to change the course of the battle.

During the next six months, Royal Navy aircraft carriers mounted eight further operations to deliver Spitfires to Malta. A total of 230 of these fighters reached the island, sufficient to maintain the strength of the force at an effective level. In October 1942, following the Allied victory at El Alamein in Egypt, the siege of Malta was finally lifted. Never again would the island face as deadly a threat as in the spring of 1942.

The flight to Malta

Plt Off Mike LeBas of No 601 Squadron piloted one of the Malta-bound Spitfires launched from *USS Wasp* on 20 April 1942. Once airborne, his first priority was to join his formation as soon as he could, as he recalled:

"High above and in front of me, Bisdee [Sqn Ldr John Bisdee, the squadron CO] took his aircraft in a wide orbit round the carrier so that I and the pilots behind me could get into position in formation as rapidly as possible. Once we had formed up, the 12 Spitfires turned due east for our new home.

"When at our cruising altitude of 10,000 ft we throttled back to 2,050 rpm to get the most out of each gallon of fuel. At first the skies were clear of cloud and to the south of us we could make out the reddish-brown peaks of the mountain range which ran along the Algerian coast. As we settled down for the long flight, boredom began to set in and I remember being worried in case I lost concentration and would not be alert if we came under attack. The sun climbed higher and higher in front of us, disconcertingly bright. At the same time, the ground haze thickened until it swallowed up the mountains which had provided a useful check on our navigation. Now there was no alternative but to continue on our compass heading, comforted only by the even drone of our Merlin engines.

"Things were to get worse before they got better. As we continued eastwards cloud began to build up beneath us, hiding the sea and our important turning point at Cap Bon. About half an hour before we were due to reach Malta we expected to be in VHF range, so Bisdee broke radio silence and called up for a homing. After a short pause a voice came up in good English and gave us a north-easterly heading to fly. Had we followed the instructions we would have been in trouble but, by a stroke of good luck, the cloud beneath us started to break up and we could see the sea again. Out to port was the Italian-held island of Pantelleria, which gave us a useful navigational fix. It was clear that the homing instructions had come from an enemy station and we ignored them. Bisdee led us in a turn to the south-east to regain our proper track.

"Just as were passing Pantelleria I nearly had my own personal disaster. Without warning, my engine suddenly cut out. I thought: 'Oh God, this is it.' I decided that if I could not get it re-started I would glide over to the island and bail out. I jettisoned the drop tank to clean up the aircraft for the glide, and then it occurred to me that perhaps the tank had run dry. So I switched over to my almost-full main tank and to my great relief the engine re-started without difficulty. I opened the throttle and regained my place in the formation.

"After Pantelleria the skies cleared up completely. My first sight of Malta was the cloud of dust towering over the island after the morning visit by the Luftwaffe. Now my great worry was that after three hours in our cramped cockpits, stiff and with sore backsides, we should not be in good shape if we had to fight our way in. Fortunately for us, however, the Germans had gone home by the time we got there and we had no trouble getting down."

Following the launch of the Spitfires from the flight deck, the engines of those in the hangar were started and the aircraft were brought up one by one on the lift to follow them. The move required slick timing, as this photograph shows. As the Spitfire in the foreground is about to begin its take-off, the aircraft ahead of it can be seen climbing away, just above the starboard wing. Meanwhile, the lift is already descending for the next aircraft.

The route to Malta flown by the Spitfires during the reinforcement operation on 20 April 1942.

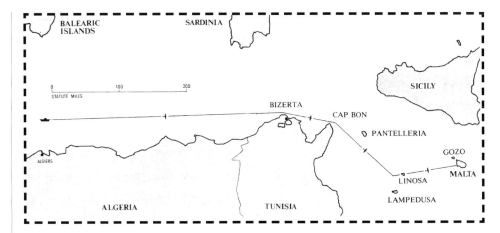

Scene on the flight deck of USS *Wasp* on the morning of 9 May 1942 as the carrier prepares to launch her Spitfires. In the background, also preparing to launch Spitfires, is HMS *Eagle*. In this, the largest reinforcement operation of all, the two carriers launched a total of 64 Spitfires of which 60 reached the island.

Next stop Malta!

After becoming airborne from USS *Wasp*, Plt Off Jerry Smith found that his 90 gal ferry tank would not feed properly. After the rest of the Spitfires had taken off, and despite the fact that his fighter lacked an arrester hook, Smith landed back on *Wasp*. For that feat the Canadian pilot was awarded a set of honorary US Navy pilot's wings.

As the USS *Wasp* sailed past Gibraltar on her way out of the Mediterranean, Jerry Smith prepared to make his second take-off from the carrier. He landed at the British base to await the next Malta reinforcement operation. The determined pilot was killed in action in the following August.

A flight of Spitfire Vs of No 249 Squadron on patrol over Malta.

Deliveries of Spitfires from aircraft carriers to Malta, 1942

Date	Operation	Carrier	No taking off	No arriving
7 March	*Spotter*	HMS *Eagle*	15	15
21 March	*Picket I*	HMS *Eagle*	9	9
29 March	*Picket II*	HMS *Eagle*	7	7
20 April	*Calendar*	USS *Wasp*	47	46
9 May	*Bowery*	USS *Wasp* and HMS *Eagle*	64	60
18 May	*LB*	HMS *Eagle*	17	17
3 June	*Style*	HMS *Eagle*	31	27
9 June	*Salient*	HMS *Eagle*	32	32
16 July	*Pinpoint*	HMS *Eagle*	32	31
21 July	*Insect*	HMS *Eagle*	30	28
11 August	*Bellows*	HMS *Furious*	38	37
17 August	*Baritone*	HMS *Furious*	32	29
24 October	*Train*	HMS *Furious*	31	29

From time to time the Luftwaffe renewed its attacks on the airfields of Malta. This Spitfire has been caught in the blast of an exploding bomb and wrecked.

Spitfire Vs of No 126 Squadron at readiness at Luqa, Malta, in the summer of 1942.

9 NEW SPITFIRE VARIANTS

WHEN the Focke-Wulf Fw 190 entered service with the *Luftwaffe* in the autumn of 1941 it demonstrated a clear margin of superiority over the Spitfire V, which formed the backbone of the RAF's day fighter squadrons. This was a worrying development for Fighter Command.

Fortunately for the RAF pilots the solution to the problem was close at hand. Earlier in the year Rolls-Royce received an order to design and build a new variant of the Merlin engine to provide enhanced high-altitude performance for bombers. The basis for the new engine was the Merlin 45, the same engine that powered the Spitfire V but fitted with two supercharger blowers in series, one feeding into the other. Between the outlet of the first blower and the inlet of the second was an intercooler to reduce the temperature of the fuel/air charge and thereby increase its density.

The two-stage supercharger had a dramatic effect on the Merlin's high altitude performance. At 30,000 ft the Merlin 45 with the single-stage supercharger developed a maximum of about 720 hp. At the same altitude, the modified engine with the two-stage supercharger developed about 1,020 hp. The huge improvement in engine performance prompted the obvious question: could the new version of the Merlin be adapted for the Spitfire?

It could indeed. The new Merlin variant for fighters, the Mk 61, was installed in a Spitfire test bed. Flight tests confirmed the huge improvement in performance compared with the Mk V. The modified fighter recorded a maximum level speed of 391 mph at 15,900 ft, 414 mph at 27,200 ft and 354 mph at 40,000 ft. The rate of climb was far superior to that of the Spitfire V and the fighter's service ceiling was estimated at 41,800 ft.

The promise of greatly improved performance from the Merlin 61 engine spawned the development of three new Spitfire fighter variants, the Mks VII, VIII and IX. The Spitfire VII was a dedicated high-altitude fighter with a pressurised cabin. Based on the earlier Mk VI, it too had pointed wing tips which increased the span by 3 ft 4 ins and increased the wing area by 6.5 sq ft. To provide sufficient fuel for a combat climb to 40,000 ft, possibly followed by a tail chase, the internal fuel capacity of the Mk VII was increased to 124 gal – 40 per cent more than previous versions of the Spitfire. The airframe of the Mk VII was redesigned and strengthened to cope with the extra weight. To reduce drag, this version was fitted with a retractable tail wheel. The second new variant, the Mk VIII, was a general purpose fighter similar to the Mk VII but without the complication of the pressurised cabin.

It would take several months to re-tool the production lines to build the Mk VIIs and Mk VIIIs in quantity, yet the Fw 190 menace remained. To counter it the RAF needed an interim Spitfire version powered by the Merlin 61 engine which could be brought into service much earlier. That variant, designated the Spitfire IX, was essentially a Mk V with strengthened engine bearers and other critical parts and a modified system of underwing radiators. The other changes were kept to the minimum necessary for the new fighter to perform reasonably effectively. The airframe of the Mk IX was not fully stressed for operations at its greater all-up weight, 875 lbs heavier than the Mk V. But in wartime risks have to be taken on the grounds of operational expediency and no red-blooded fighter pilot would willingly forgo the higher performance of the Mk IX in favour of the relatively slow Mk V.

Mk IX Spitfires began coming off the production lines in June 1942. Initially they represented a small proportion of the Spitfire force yet they had an almost immediate impact on the situation over northern Europe. In combat it was almost impossible to distinguish a Spitfire IX from a Mk V and *Luftwaffe* pilots could never be certain which variant was confronting them. As a result

SPITFIRE IX VERSUS FOCKE-WULF FW 190 A-3

In July 1942 the Spitfire IX was flown in a comparative trial against a captured Fw 190. Considering that they were quite different aircraft, the similarities in their performance were remarkable, as the following excerpts from the official trials report show.

Comparative Speeds: The Fw 190 was compared with a fully operational Spitfire IX for speed and manoeuvrability at heights up to 25,000 ft. The Spitfire IX at most heights was slightly superior in speed to the Fw 190 and the approximate differences in speeds at various heights were that at:

- 2,000 ft the Fw 190 was 7 to 8 mph faster than the Spitfire IX
- 5,000 ft the Fw 190 and the Spitfire IX were approximately the same
- 8,000 ft the Spitfire IX was 8 mph faster than the Fw 190
- 15,000 ft the Spitfire IX was 5 mph faster
- 18,000 ft the Fw 190 was 3 mph faster than the Spitfire IX
- 21,000 ft the Fw 190 and the Spitfire IX were approximately the same
- 25,000 ft the Spitfire IX was 5 to 7 mph faster than the Fw 190

Climb: During comparative climbs at various heights up to 23,000 ft with both aircraft flying under maximum continuous climbing conditions, little difference was found between the two aircraft although on the whole the Spitfire IX was slightly better. Above 22,000 ft the Fw 190's climb was falling off rapidly, whereas that of the Spitfire IX was increasing.

Dive: The Fw 190 was faster than the Spitfire IX in a dive, particularly during the initial stage. This superiority was not as marked as with the Spitfire VB.

Manoeuvrability: The Fw 190 was more manoeuvrable than the Spitfire IX except in turning circles when it was out-turned without difficulty. The Fw 190's superior rate of roll enabled it to avoid the Spitfire IX if attacked when in a turn by flicking over into a diving turn in the opposition direction. As with the Spitfire VB, the Spitfire IX had great difficulty in following this manoeuvre.

The Spitfire IX's worst heights for fighting the Fw 190 were found to be between 18,000 and 22,000 ft and below 3,000 ft. At these heights the Fw 190 was a little faster. The Fw 190's initial acceleration was better than the Spitfire IX's under all conditions of flight except in level flight at the altitudes where the Spitfire had a speed advantage. Then, provided the Spitfire was cruising at high speed, there was little to choose between the acceleration of the two aircraft.

The general impression gained by the pilots taking part in the trials was that the Spitfire IX compared favourably with the Fw 190. Provided the Spitfire had the initiative, it undoubtedly had a good chance of shooting down the Fw 190.

---

they became markedly less aggressive and RAF fighter losses fell.

One further development needs to be mentioned at this point: the Spitfire Mk XI reconnaissance version. During 1942 deployment of the latest variants of the Messerschmitt Bf 109 G and the Fw 190 A made life increasingly hazardous for the reconnaissance Spitfires. The answer was to develop a PR variant combining the Merlin 61 engine, the strengthened airframe structure and retractable tail wheel of the of the Spitfire VIII and the integral wing fuel tanks of the PR Mk IV. This resulted in the Mk XI, which entered service early in 1943.

For the year and a half that followed this variant's superb high-altitude performance would provide it with a high degree of immunity from fighter attack. The Mk XI replaced all previous unarmed reconnaissance versions of the Spitfire in front-line units.

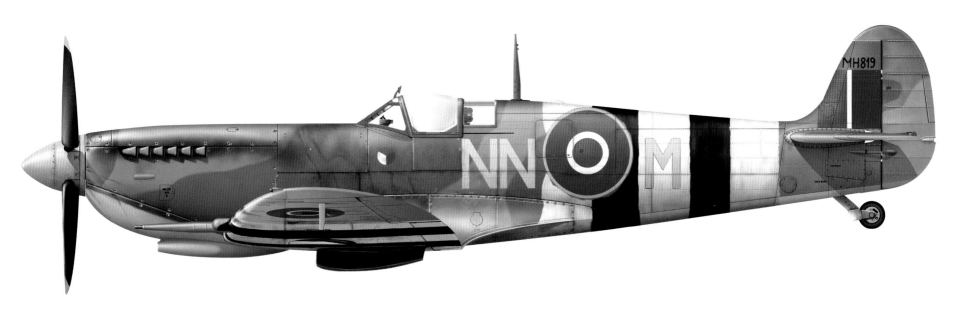

Supermarine Spitfire Mk IX, MH819, NN-M of 310 Squadron, No 134 Wing 1944
Note the crudely applied invasion stripes and repositioned serial number above the fin flash. Camouflaged in Dark Green and Ocean Grey upper surfaces with Medium Sea Grey under surfaces.

A Spitfire Mk IX of 310 Squadron at Apuldram in Holland, 1944. The aircraft is being levelled off in preparation for gun harmonisation.

The Spitfire VII was optimised for the high-altitude interceptor role and featured an extended span wing with pointed tips, and a pressurised cabin.

The Spitfire VIII entered service after the Mk IX. The entire production run of this variant was shipped overseas and served in the Middle East and the Far East. This example belongs to No 457 Squadron RAAF, which operated from Northern Australia into the mid-western Pacific region from 1943 onwards.

Supermarine Spitfire HF Mk VIII. A58-615, ZP-Y, flown by WC Glen Cooper of 457 Squadron RAAF, Livingstone, Australia 1943
Camouflage is Dark Green and Ocean Grey upper surfaces over Medium Sea Grey lower surfaces. The wing leading edges carry white theatre identification markings.

A Spitfire Mk IX of the 309th Fighter Squadron, 31st Fighter Group, which operated in Tunisia in 1943. The aircraft is named *Thurla Mae III*.

Spitfire Mk IXs of the 309th Fighter Squadron, 31st Fighter Group, are lined up before the unit re-equipped with the P-51 Mustangs in the background. The pilots missed the Spitfire's pleasant handling characteristics, but the Mustang's much greater range enabled it to take the fight deep into enemy territory.

'Yank in a Spit'– Ex-No. 121 Sqn pilot Don Willis in his Spitfire Mk. VB, BM590, AV-R, was made Operations Officer of the 335th FS, following the unit's absorption into the USAAF. Having served in the RAF since late 1941, Willis was a vastly experienced pilot who wore no less than four sets of wings on his uniform - Finnish Air Force, Royal Norwegian Air Force, RAF and USAAF. Almost certainly the first US-based volunteer pilot of the Second World War, he had trained with the Finns during the Russo-Finnish war of late 1939, then joined the Royal Norwegian Air Force when Germany invaded in April 1940. Escaping to the UK when Norway fell, Willis eventually made it into the RAF and then to 121 Sqn. Tour expired in 1943, he returned to action the following year, but was shot down in a P-38 and made a POW until the war's end.

Supermarine Spitfire Mk Vc ER570, WD-Q flown by Major Robert Levine, 4th Fighter Squadron, 52nd Fighter Group, La Sebala, Tunisia, June 1943
Major Robert Levine's aircraft illustrates the early markings of the Group, which included the American flag on the fuselage and non-standard code letters. Major Levine scored three confirmed kills and one probable in this well-maintained Spitfire.

Captain Robert Levine's Spitfire Mk Vc at Bône, Algeria, January 1943.

Major Robert Levine of the 4th Fighter Squadron, proudly pointing out a Swastika, indicating his first aerial victory, 8 January 1943.

Spitfire XIs of the 10th Photo Group, US Eighth Army Air Force. The unit operated this variant on photographic reconnaissance missions over occupied Europe. Note the re-profiled lower cowling, peculiar to this mark, which housed an enlarged oil tank.

Spitfire XI of No 16 Squadron displays its invasion markings. Fitted with the 60 Series Merlin engine, it was the most-used reconnaissance variant during the mid-war period.

Mark XI of No 400 (Canadian) Squadron taxies out over a flooded airfield in northern Europe early in 1945.

A Mark XI of No 541 Squadron shows to good advantage the split pair of vertical camera windows in the rear lower fuselage. These aircraft could operate up to 40,000 feet and relied upon speed as their means of escape. They had a maximum speed in the region of 422 mph and a range of 1,360 miles.

Spitfire Mk. VIII, JG204, was a tropical trials aircraft which underwent extensive testing at Farnborough before the mark was cleared for service in the Far East. The picture was taken in the UK, and the machine is in Mediterranean colours.

A captured Spitfire XI of the 'Wanderzirkus Rosarius', a unit formed to tour German fighter units, displaying captured British and American aircraft. The aircraft is an ex No 412 (RCAF) Squadron machine, and was lost in mid 1944. It is seen here being examined with much interest by Luftwaffe fighter pilots, possibly from JG 27.

Three Spitfire Vs were modified as floatplanes for a planned operation in the Mediterranean against German transport aircraft carrying supplies to the garrisons on the various occupied Greek islands. In the event the operation was cancelled and the Spitfire floatplane never saw action. These photographs were taken over the Great Bitter Lake in Egypt during pilot training for the aborted operation.

Late production Spitfire Mark IXs and XVIs featured cut-down fuselages and bubble canopies, as seen on this Mark XVI of No 17 Squadron.

Spitfire XVIs of No 74 Squadron operating from Schijndel in Holland during the closing stages of the war in Europe.

The Spitfire XVI was similar to
the Mk IX but was powered by
the Merlin 266 engine built under
licence by the Packard Car
Company in the USA.

Members of 6308 Servicing Echelon of 131 Airfield HQ of the Polish Air Force and RAF Regiment units of 84 Group 2nd TAF stationed at the emergency airfield in Chailey, Sussex, during July 1944 carry out maintenance work on a Spitfire coded JH–V of 317 Squadron. Note the pilot's seat in the foreground.

Top Gun Spitfire

'Johnnie' Johnson, Kenley Wing, 1943.

The Royal Air Force did not record victory claims of individual aircraft, so there is no official record of the top-scoring Spitfire. However, Spitfire Mark IX EN398 is probably the strongest contender for that title.

In February 1943 this brand new aircraft was delivered from the Supermarine airfield at Chattis Hill near Andover, to RAF Kenley. Kenley was the home of Canadian Fighter Wing comprising Nos 403 and 416 Squadrons with Mark IX Spitfires, and Nos 411 and 421 Squadrons with Mark Vs.

At the same time 'Johnnie' Johnson, newly promoted to Wing Commander, was posted to Kenley to take command of the Wing. At that time his victory score stood at 7 enemy aircraft destroyed plus 2 shared, 4 probably destroyed and 5 enemy aircraft damaged.

Johnson looked over some newly delivered Spitfires to choose his personal aircraft, and his eyes fell on EN398. As he told this author:

'I found the engineer officer and together we had a look at her, gleaming and bright in a new spring coat of camouflage paint. Later I took her up for a few aerobatics to get the feel of her, for this was the first time I had flown a [Spitfire Mark] IX. She seemed very fast, the engine was sweet and she responded to the controls as only a thoroughbred can. I decided that she should be mine, and I never had occasion to regret the choice.'

Having selected his personal mount Johnson had his initials, 'JE-J', painted on the fuselage in place of the usual squadron code letters. He also had the fighter's weapons re-harmonised to suit his style of air fighting. The standard harmonisation for the Spitfires' guns spread the rounds from the cannon and machine guns across a circle a few yards across. That gave pilots of average ability the best chance of scoring hits. Johnson's shooting skills were far above the average, however. He had his weapons adjusted to converge on a single point ahead of the aircraft, to inflict maximum destruction at that point.

During March 1943 Johnson led the Kenley Wing over northern France on four separate operations, flying EN398 each time. And on each occasion he returned without having fired his guns in anger.

Things went differently on Johnson's next mission, however, on 3 April. That afternoon his two Mark IX squadrons provided top cover for Typhoons attacking Abbeville airfield. There was a vigorous enemy reaction and Johnson manoeuvred his squadrons into a position above and behind a force of Focke-Wulf Fw 190s. In the 'bounce' that followed Johnson

hauled EN398 into a firing position behind a German fighter. His first burst missed so he made a brief correction and fired again. Cannon shells thudded into the Focke-Wulf and it began to burn. Johnson gave it another long burst, then broke away in a steep climbing turn. During that action, the Kenley pilots claimed five Fw 190s shot down, one probably destroyed and one damaged, for the loss of one of their number.

Each Spitfire had an idiosyncrasy, large or small. As Johnson became familiar with EN398 he found that it had one also. As he commented to the author:

'The aeroplane always flew with the turn needle of the turn-and-bank indicator a little bit to one side, even when flying straight and level and on an absolutely even keel. That was disconcerting sometimes when you were flying on instruments, because if you corrected for it you would swing to one side. Changing the turn-and-bank instrument did not cure it – it must have been something to do with the aeroplane. I even took the aeroplane to Eastleigh and had Jeffrey Quill fly it. I asked if he could have it put right. I left it at the works for a few days but they couldn't cure the problem.'

The fault was so small, and the fighter handled so beautifully in every other respect, that the fighter ace decided he would live with the problem.

By the end of June Johnson had added eleven victories and two shared victories to his score and that of EN398, now established as his personal Spitfire. Only he flew it, unless for some reason he was away from the unit. That occurred on 20 June, when Squadron Leader Robert McNair flew EN398 in action and was credited with the destruction of an Fw 190.

After a spot of leave Johnson resumed operations on 15 July, and in the next four weeks his run of successes in EN398 continued with two Bf 109s destroyed, two damaged and two more shared. Near the end of August EN398 went to Air Service Training Ltd at Hamble to receive a replacement engine. On 5 September Johnson was again in action in EN398 and credited with a Messerschmitt Bf 109 damaged. He flew her on operations on the 6th and twice on the 8th, but had no further contact with enemy aircraft. A few days later he relinquished command of the Wing to take up a staff appointment at No 11 Group Headquarters.

During his six-month operational tour Johnson shot down twelve enemy aircraft in EN398, shared in the destruction of five more and inflicted damage on a further seven. In addition Squadron Leader Robert McNair had flown the Spitfire on one occasion when he shot down an Fw 190. Thus, adding up the half shares in victories, EN398 can be credited with the destruction of fifteen enemy aircraft and for causing damage to seven more. It never once returned early from a mission due to a technical failure, and in Johnson's skilful hands it never suffered so much as a scratch in combat.

By today's standards, EN398 would certainly deserve to go into honourable retirement in an air museum. Alas, it was not to be. As Johnson moved to take up his staff appointment, life for his once-pampered Spitfire went rapidly downhill.

Two weeks later, while serving with No 421 Squadron, EN398 suffered damage in an accident and went to a repair unit for several months. From there, in March 1944, it went into a holding unit to await re-allocation to an operational unit. By that time the production of new

Johnson with the top scoring Spitfire Mk. IXB, JE-J, EN398, his personal aircraft for most of 1943.

Spitfires exceeded losses, and the newest Spitfires to arrive at the holding unit were the first to be issued. That meant EN398 went progressively down the queue and it was still at the Support Unit when the war in Europe ended.

'Johnnie' Johnson ended the war with the rank of Group Captain, credited with the destruction of 34 enemy aircraft destroyed and shared destroyed, 3 and 2 shared probably destroyed, 10 and 3 shared damaged and 1 shared destroyed on the ground. All of those victories were scored while flying Spitfires, making him the top-scoring Spitfire ace and the second highest scoring British Commonwealth ace.

Meanwhile, EN398's descent to oblivion continued. In May 1945 it went to a training unit at Ouston in Northumberland, where it suffered ill-treatment from novice pilots ignorant of its distinguished past. In March 1946 it made its last flight, to a maintenance unit at High Ercal, Shropshire, where it went into long-term storage. Its end came suddenly in October 1949 when, without ceremony, remorse or even comment, it was sold to Henry Bath & Son Ltd and was carted off for scrap.

Left: DP 845, the prototype
Griffon-powered Spitfire.
First designated as a Mk IV,
this aircraft eventually became
the Mk XII prototype.

SHORTLY before the outbreak of the Second World War, Rolls-Royce engineers began work on a new aero engine based on the 36-litre 12-cylinder sprint engine which had powered the Supermarine racing seaplanes. The new engine, named the Griffon, was designed to replace the 27-litre Merlin in some aircraft types, including the Spitfire. By some inspired juggling of components the designers kept the Griffon's frontal area within 6 per cent, its length to within 3 in and its weight to within 600 lbs of the equivalent figures for the Merlin. The Griffon II engine, with a single stage supercharger, developed 1,735 hp for take-off.

Supermarine received an order for 100 Griffon Spitfires and this variant entered service as the Mk XII. It had a maximum speed of 372 mph at 5,700 ft, increasing to 397 mph at 18,000 ft. Production Mk XIIs were optimised for low-altitude operations and had clipped wings to improve rate of roll. Compared with the Mk IX, the Spitfire XII was 14 mph faster at sea level.

To exploit to the full the Griffon's potential it was necessary to install a two-stage supercharger, as had been the case with the Merlin 61. Thus modified, the engine was designated the Griffon 61, rated at 2,035 hp at 7,000 ft. The first Spitfire variant fitted with the new engine was the Mk XIV, with a maximum speed of 446 mph at 25,400 ft. This was a converted Mk VIII and as it was not fully stressed to carry the

extra weight, it needed to be treated carefully. Nevertheless, pilots who flew this and other Spitfire variants rated the Mk XIV very highly. The consensus of opinion was that it was the most formidable combat fighter of the entire Spitfire breed. The Mk XIV entered service with No 610 Squadron in January 1944.

Early in 1944 the RAF issued an urgent requirement for a reconnaissance version of the Spitfire powered by the Griffon 61 engine. Driving this demand was the fear that the *Luftwaffe* was about to deploy large numbers of high-performance jet fighters. If that happened there were dangerous times ahead for the reconnaissance

Two fighter squadrons, Nos 41
(depicted) and 91, operated the
Spitfire XII. These aircraft had
clipped wings and a single-stage
supercharger for optimum
performance at low altitude.

Spitfire Mk XII EB-D of No 41 Squadron. They used these aircraft to counter the hit-and-run Fw 190 attacks on the south coast towns.

Mk XIV Spitfire of No 402 (Canadian) Squadron fitted with a Griffon 61 engine with two-stage supercharger. This version entered service in the spring of 1944 and many pilots judged it to be the most effective high-altitude air superiority variant of the Spitfire.

SPITFIRE XIV VERSUS MESSERSCHMITT BF 109 G-6

Early in 1944 the Air Fighting Development Unit at Duxford ran a comparative trial pitting the Spitfire XIV against a captured Messerschmitt Bf 109 G, the latest sub-type of the German fighter then available. The official trials report showed that in terms of **maximum speed** the Spitfire XIV was 40 mph faster at all heights except near 16,000 ft, where it was only 10 mph faster.

The report also showed that at 16,000 ft the **maximum climb** rate of the two aircraft was identical; otherwise the Spitfire XIV out-climbed the 109 G. The zoom climb was practically identical when the climb was made without opening the throttle. Climbing at full throttle, the Spitfire XIV drew away from the Bf 109 G quite easily.

Other findings were as follows:

Dive: During the initial part of the dive, the Bf 109 G pulled away slightly but when a speed of 380 mph was reached the Spitfire XIV began to gain on the 109 G.

Turning Circle: The Spitfire XIV easily out-turned the Bf 109 G in either direction.

Rate of Roll: The Spitfire XIV rolled much more quickly. The report concluded: *"The Spitfire XIV is superior to the Me 109 G in every respect."*

A Bf 109 G-6/R6, similar to the type that was flown in comparison trials with the Spitfire XIV, as well as a Spitfire IX and Mustang III (P-51C).

Spitfire census: fighter variants on charge on 1 June 1944

On this date, less than a week before the Allied invasion of Normandy, the RAF had a total of 3,748 Spitfire fighter variants on charge. This figure comprised Mk V, VII, VIII, IX, XII and XIV fighters of which 1,980 were assigned to front-line squadrons and 606 were held at Aircraft Storage Units ready for immediate issue. The table below gives the breakdown of the figures in the various categories, by mark:

Mark	V	VII	VIII	IX	XII	XIV
With home squadrons	278	62	-	724	22	56
With overseas squadrons	282	-	204	352	-	-
Undergoing repair or in long-term storage	507	-	295	370	-	-
Held at aircraft storage units	103	43	28	397	21	14
Totals	**1,170**	**105**	**527**	**1,843**	**43**	**70**

force. The answer was the Spitfire Mk XIX, which combined the Griffon 61 with the extra internal fuel tanks and camera layout of the Mk XI. This variant entered service with No 542 Squadron in May 1944. It would become the definitive reconnaissance variant of the Spitfire.

The late production Mk XIXs were fitted with pressurised cabins, enabling pilots to exploit their superb high-altitude capability. In post-war RAF air defence exercises, Spitfire XIXs photographed targets from altitudes as high as 49,000 ft. Not until the deployment of the second generation of jet fighters, the swept-wing F-86 Sabre and the Soviet MiG-15, was there a fighter with the performance to intercept a Spitfire XIX flying at its maximum attainable altitude. The reconnaissance Mk XIX would soldier on longer than any other Spitfire variant and the last one passed out of front-line RAF service in 1954.

This Spitfire XIV was fitted experimentally with skis to enable it to operate from a snow-covered runway in Canada. Once the aircraft was off the ground, the skis would fall away.

IMPROVING THE BREED

The Spitfire underwent many hundreds of modifications during the war to improve its combat capability or reduce its failings. Three important changes incorporated in Spitfire fighter variants built after the autumn of 1944 deserve mention: the fitting of the 'E' type wing and revised armament; the bubble canopy, together with the redesigned and cut-back rear fuselage; and the installation of the Gyro Gun Sight. These modifications, described in more detail below, were applied to the three variants then in large-scale production: the Mks IX, XIV and XVI.

The 'E' type wing and armament: Until mid-1944 most Spitfire fighter variants carried a standard armament of two 20 mm Hispano cannon and four .303 inch Browning machine guns. By then the rifle-calibre weapon had limited effectiveness as the majority of enemy aircraft carried armour protection for their vulnerable areas. To overcome that failing the Spitfire wing was redesigned to carry a .5 inch Browning heavy machine gun in place of the two .303 inch weapons on each side. The .5 inch weapon delivered a much heavier penetrative punch than the smaller calibre gun and enhanced the fighter's effectiveness for both air-to-air and air-to-ground firing.

The bubble canopy: When one fighter pilot shot down another, the victim had usually failed to see his assailant in time to take evasive action. Any modification that helped prevent such surprise attacks therefore enhanced the fighter's operational value. In the case of the Spitfire, the answer was to cut back the rear fuselage behind the cockpit and fit a bubble canopy. In 1943 a Spitfire VIII was so modified and sent to the Air Fighting Development Unit to gauge the opinions of pilots with combat experience. They were hugely impressed with the change and the official report on the modification stated:

"This is an enormous improvement over the standard Spitfire rear view. The pilot can see quite easily round to his fin and past it, almost to the further edge of the tailplane, ie if he looks over his left shoulder he can practically see to the starboard tip of the tail. By banking the aircraft slightly during weaving action, the downward view to the rear is opened up well . . . Owing to the very great improvement in all-round search view, particularly to the rear, the omission of the rear view mirror is not considered to be of any disadvantage to pilots flying with this new hood."

From the latter part of 1944 all new production Spitfire Mk IXs, XIVs and XVIs were fitted with bubble canopies. These aircraft went into action immediately and became popular with pilots.

The Gyro Gun Sight: It may sound obvious but the effectiveness of a fighter's cannon and machine gun armament depends entirely on the pilot's ability to aim them accurately. For most of the war RAF fighters carried the simple GM2 reflector gun sight which provided an illuminated fixed aiming point in the centre of the reflector glass, surrounded by a circle to assist in judging the deflection angle required when engaging a manoeuvring or crossing target. The ability to judge that deflection angle accurately was the major factor determining which pilots became aces and which were also-rans. Following some inspired work by scientists at the Royal Aircraft Establishment at Farnborough, the Mark II Gyro Gun Sight entered production at the end of 1943. During a turning fight, a gyroscope measured the fighter's rate of turn and then moved the position of the sighting graticule on the sight to show the amount of aim-off required to hit the target.

Once fighter pilots had learned the new sight's foibles, the accuracy of their deflection shooting improved dramatically. During 1944 an analysis of 130 combats by Spitfire IXs fitted with fixed-graticule sights revealed that there had been 34 shoot-downs – 26 per cent of the total. In the same period, one squadron of Spitfire IXs was equipped with the new gun sight and participated in 38 combats, gaining 19 shoot-downs – 50 per cent of the total. At a stroke, the new sight had almost doubled the effectiveness of air-to-air gunnery.

Yet many ace pilots did not want it. It restricted visibility in the vitally important sector in front of the aircraft and it was necessary to track the target for several seconds while the new sight calculated the deflection angle. Those exceptional pilots could judge the amount of deflection required at a glance and for them the disadvantages of the Gyro Gun Sight outweighed its advantages. Yet, by definition, exceptional pilots comprised only a small proportion of the force. The capability of a fighter force as a whole depended on the shooting ability of the average pilot, not that of the aces.

During the war's final months, Allied piston-engined fighters often confronted the much faster German jet types. It was the improvement in air-to-air gunnery which helped to compensate for the huge difference in performance and enabled the Allied air forces to maintain air superiority.

Spitfire XVIII fighters undergoing final assembly at High Post, 1945.

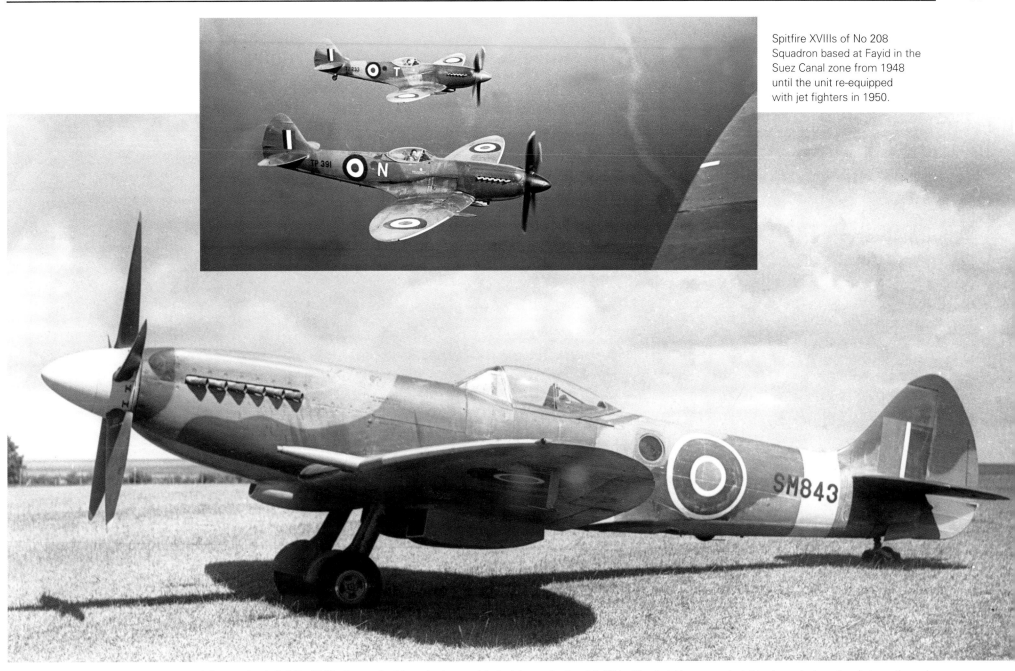

Spitfire XVIIIs of No 208 Squadron based at Fayid in the Suez Canal zone from 1948 until the unit re-equipped with jet fighters in 1950.

A factory-fresh Spitfire XVIII. Externally this variant resembled a late production Mk XIV with a bubble canopy but it had a redesigned and strengthened airframe to restore its load factor.

Heavily weathered Mk XVIII of No 28 Squadron pictured at Kai Tak, Hong Kong, in 1950. The aircraft displays the black and white identification bands on the rear fuselage and above and below the wings, introduced soon after the start of the Korean War.

Supermarine Spitfire Mk XVIII, H of 28 Squadron, Kai Tak, Hong Kong, 1950
Camouflaged in Dark Green and Ocean Grey upper surfaces with Medium Sea Grey under surfaces.

The Griffon-powered Mk XIX
was the definitive Spitfire
reconnaissance variant. It entered
service in 1944 and remained
in front-line service in the RAF
until 1954.

12 FINAL SPITFIRE FIGHTER VARIANTS

Left: With the Mark 21 and subsequent variations of the Spitfire, the previous system of designating successive variants with Roman numerals was superseded by Arabic numbers. The extensively modified and strengthened PP139 served as a development prototype for the Spitfire Mk 21.

WHEN the Second World War ended the RAF had just over 1,000 Spitfires serving with its front-line units. In the months to follow this force contracted rapidly as many units disbanded and others re-equipped with jet fighters.

In the early post-war period the main production variant was the Spitfire XVIII. Externally, this fighter resembled a late production Mk XIV with a bubble canopy and a cut-back rear fuselage. But it had a redesigned and strengthened airframe and, to increase range, it carried an extra fuel tank in the rear fuselage. About 300 examples were produced and the type equipped six squadrons all serving overseas. The Mk XVIII saw action against Communist guerrillas in Malaya and in the Middle East in the clashes that preceded the foundation of the state of Israel.

To exploit to the full the power available from the two-stage supercharged Griffon 61 engine, one further major redesign of the Spitfire airframe was put in hand in 1943. This was the Spitfire 21, the 'definitive' fighter variant which introduced several design changes. The internal wing structure was reinforced and, to improve rolling performance, the ailerons were five per cent larger than those fitted to previous variants. The resultant straightening of the wing trailing edge brought about the first move away from the Spitfire's original elliptical wing shape. Initially this variant flew with pointed wing tips for optimum performance at high altitude. The armament was standardised at four 20 mm cannon.

The first production Spitfire 21, LA187, made its maiden flight on 15 March 1944 but the various alterations to the airframe brought about a marked deterioration in the Mk 21's handling characteristics. In November 1944 this aircraft underwent a handling trial at Boscombe Down, which resulted in an unflattering report.

"The rudder trimmer tab was very sensitive and required a very delicate touch to trim the aircraft for flight without yawing. This latter characteristic was accentuated by the large change of directional trim with speed, power and applied acceleration, rendering it necessary for the pilot to re-trim the aircraft frequently during manoeuvres in order to avoid what appeared to be dangerous angles of sideslip. The directional qualities of the aircraft deteriorated markedly with altitude and also noticeably with aft movement of the centre of gravity. The bad directional qualities linked up with their effect on the longitudinal control, gave rise to very peculiar corkscrew behaviour of the aircraft, particularly at high Mach numbers, and at none of the loadings tested did the pilot feel comfortable when carrying out combat manoeuvres in the region of the aircraft's optimum performance altitude (25,000 ft)."

As might be expected, this report caused a considerable stir. Tooling up was well advanced at the Castle Bromwich plant to meet orders for more than 3,000 aircraft. Every day more Mark 21s were coming off the production line, all with the same poor handling characteristics. Recalling those problems, Jeffrey Quill told the author:

"From the time I first flew the Spitfire 21 it was clear that we had a hot potato. There was too much power for the aeroplane and what was needed were much larger tail surfaces, both horizontal and vertical. The work to design and build these was already in hand but would take several months to complete. In the meantime the great production 'sausage machine' was already rolling. So the immediate problem was to make the handling of the Mk 21 in the air reasonably tolerable so that the aeroplane would be operationally viable pending the happy day when the much larger tail did become available.

"We tried all sorts of expedients: different tabs, anti-balance tabs, changes to horn-balance areas, etc. Throughout these trials very few detailed reports were written. Modifications were decided upon overnight at meetings and incorporated. I would test their effect and report on them verbally to Joe Smith and his staff and then they were adopted or discarded. This was Joe Smith's method of operation and also mine."

The task of isolating the Mk 21's faults went ahead at top priority. The root cause of the problems was over-control and in each case a modification to the flying controls provided the answer. The rudder over-control was cured by removing the balance action of the rudder trim tab. The elevator over-control was cured by reducing the gearing to the elevator trim tab by half and by fitting metal-covered elevators with rounded-off horn balances of slightly reduced area. The changes were incorporated in an early production aircraft, LA215, which then went to the Air Fighting Development Unit for testing. The unit's new test report, issued in March 1945, stated:

"The critical trimming characteristics reported on the production Spitfire 21 have been largely eliminated by the modifications carried out on the aircraft. Its handling qualities have benefited to a corresponding extent and it is now considered suitable both for instrument flying and low flying."

The Spitfire 21 was to have replaced all other variants but with the end of the war most of its contracts were cancelled and production ended after 120 aircraft had been built. The next production variant, the Mk 22, was essentially similar to the Mk 21 but had a bubble canopy and cut-back rear fuselage. Production Mk 22s also featured the redesigned and enlarged fin and tailplane mentioned by Jeffrey Quill. This greatly improved stability and handling. The majority of the 278 Mk 22s built served with the Royal Auxiliary Air Force, whose squadrons were manned by the so-called 'weekend warriors'.

Externally the final Spitfire variant, the Mk 24, closely resembled the Mk 22 but had wing fittings for the carriage of six rocket projectiles. Production of new-build Mk 24s ran to 54 units and a further 27 were converted from Mk 22s. Only one front-line fighter

Up close and personal: a Mk 21 in a firing position.

Mk 21s serving with No 41 Squadron based at Lübeck in Germany in 1946.

unit received Mk 24s, No 80 Squadron. It served initially in Germany before moving to Hong Kong in July 1949. The last RAF unit to fly Spitfires in the fighter role, it re-equipped with de Havilland Hornets in January 1952.

The photographic reconnaissance Spitfire XIX continued for a further two years before ending its front-line service in the Far East in April 1954. Although the Spitfire had now passed out of front-line service, it would continue to perform second-line tasks for a further three years. The last full-time RAF unit to operate Spitfires was the civilian-manned Meteorological Flight based at Woodvale in Cheshire. The unit's Spitfire XIXs, fitted with meteorological measuring equipment, made daily flights to high altitude to record temperature and pressure readings in each altitude band. These flights continued until June 1957, when the unit exchanged its Spitfires for Mosquitoes. This was a move which was to set the stage for an entirely new career path for Reginald Mitchell's little fighter.

A few Spitfires were fitted with contra-rotating propeller units in which two three-bladed units rotated in opposite directions. Although this change made the fighter easier to fly and a much steadier gun platform, the complex device was initially unreliable and it did not go into general service use in Spitfires.

Spitfire Mk. 21s of No 41 Squadron operating from the airfield at Lübeck shortly after the end of the war.

Right: The first production Mk. 22, PK312 is seen performing for the camera.

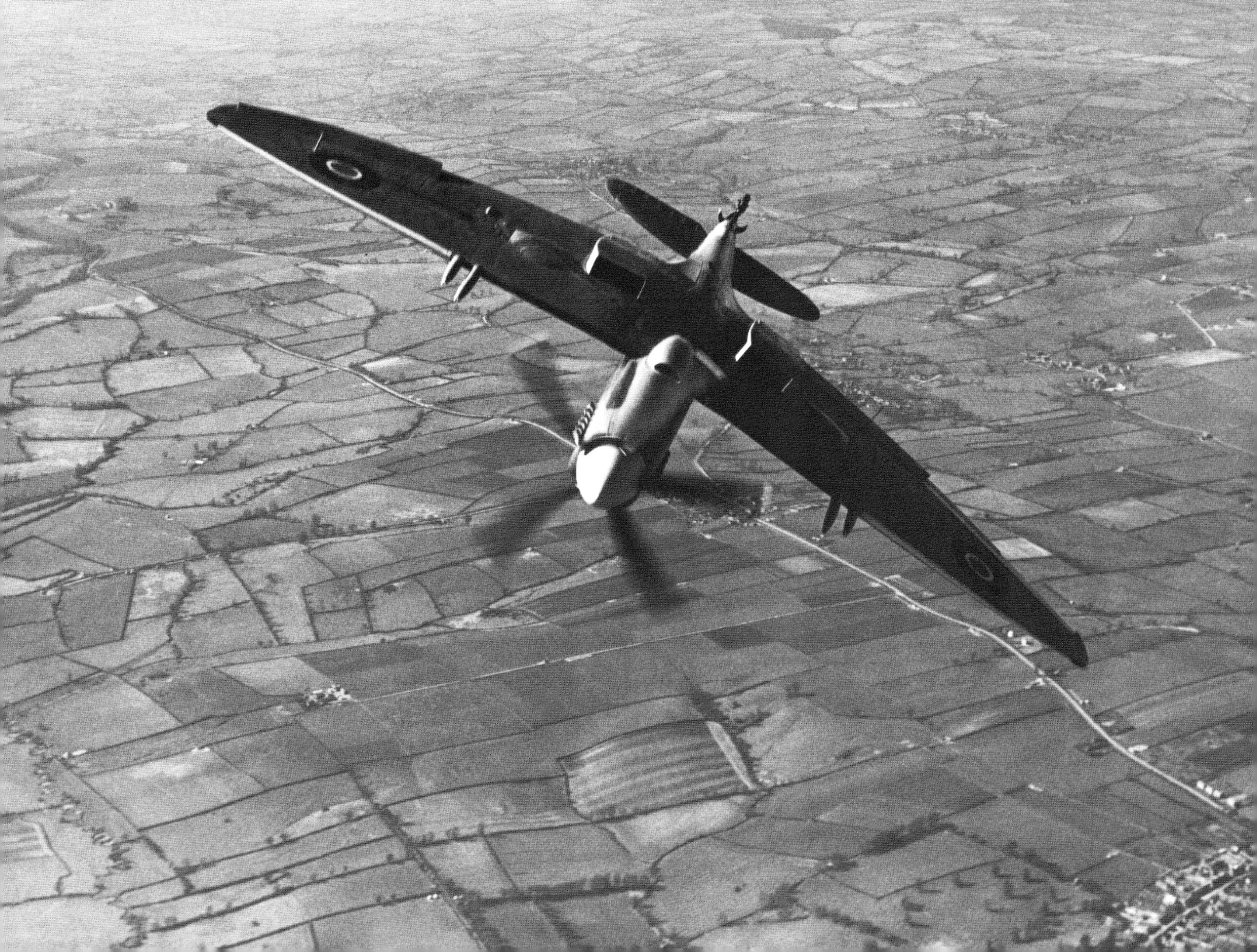

Early production Spitfire Mk 22 with the original (small-sized) Mk 21 tail surfaces.

The Spitfire Mk. 22 equipped the majority of Royal Auxiliary Air Force units during the late 1940s. This aircraft belonged to No 613 (City of Manchester) Squadron based at Ringwood, which received that variant in the summer of 1948. Note the enlarged fin and rudder seen on late production Mk. 22s.

Right: From its external appearance the final Spitfire variant, the Mk 24, was little different from the Mk 22. The main changes were the installation of two additional fuel tanks in the rear fuselage, wing fittings to carry six 3-inch rocket projectiles, and a revised electrical system. Only one regular RAF unit, No 80 Squadron, received this variant and after a brief spell in Germany, the squadron took its Mk 24s to Hong Kong.

13 SPITFIRES INTERNATIONAL, POST-WAR

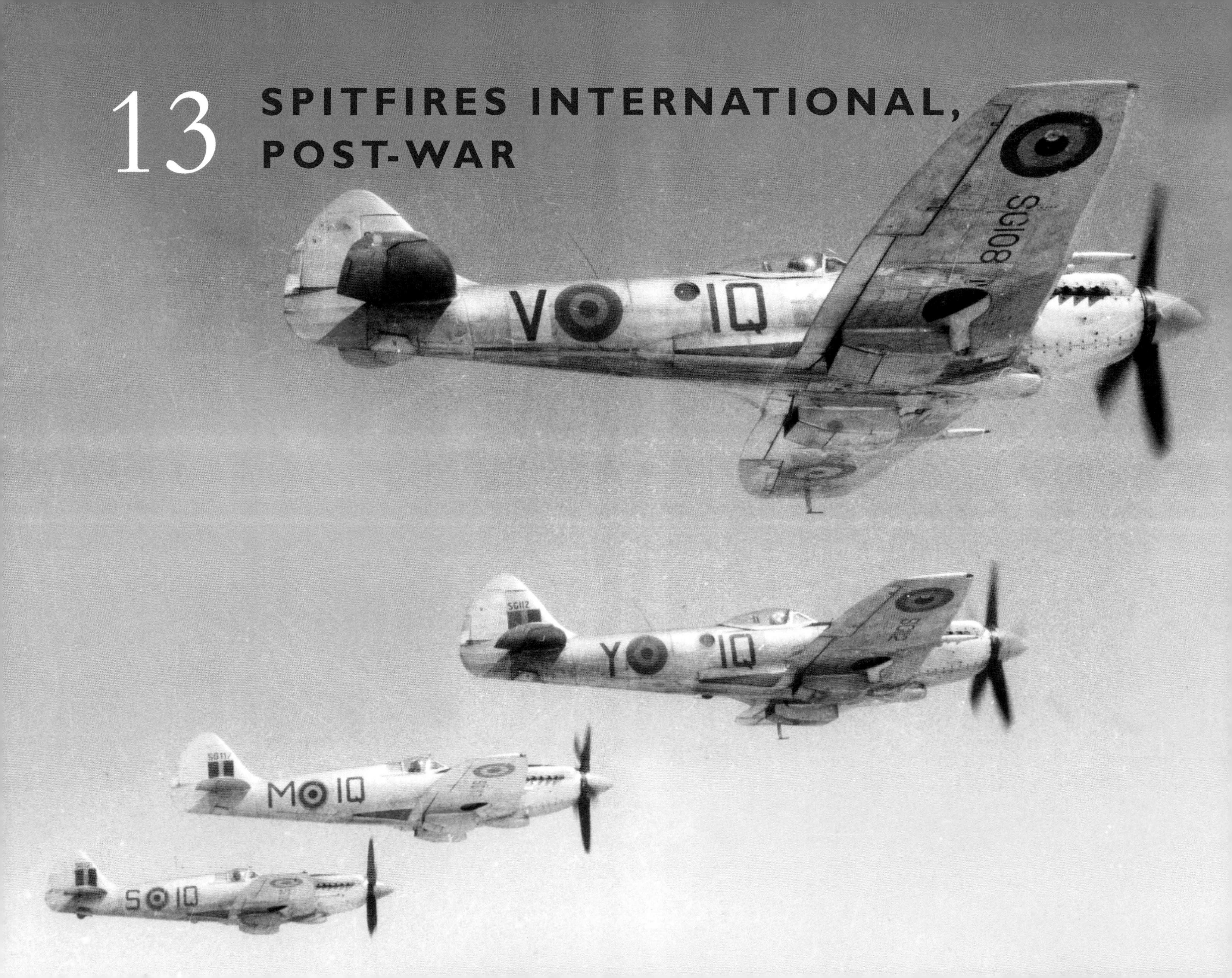

Spitfire XIVs of the Royal Belgian Air Force, which received 134 examples of this variant as well as 69 Mk IXs and XVIs.

Spitfire IX of No 322 Squadron of the Royal Dutch Air Force, based at Twente in March 1951. The service received 77 Spitfires after the war.

One of 77 examples of the Mark IX passed to the Czechoslovak Air Force after the war. Several of these aircraft were sold to the Israeli Air Force, which later passed them on to the Burmese Air Force.

Spitfire XVIII of the Royal Indian Air Force, which acquired 135 examples of this variant as well as a number of Mark XIVs and XIXs.

The Italian Air Force received 143 Spitfire IXs after the war; these examples carry the insignia of the 51° Stormo. A good number of these Spitfires were in turn sold to the emerging state of Israel in 1951, where they served for around five years before then being sold to Burma.

The Royal Swedish Air Force purchased 50 examples of the Mk XIX and during the Cold War these aircraft flew occasional clandestine missions to photograph targets in Soviet-occupied eastern Europe.

Above and below: Originally a Spitfire Mk IX, MT818 became the first prototype Tr 9, the two-seat trainer. Bought by Vickers, the conversion was carried out by them at Chilbolton and the aircraft first flew in August 1946 with B-Condition markings, 'N32' in an all-over yellow scheme (above). These trainers served with the Indian, the Dutch and the Egyptian air forces, as well as the Irish Air Corps. The photograph below shows the aircraft at the Royal Aeronautical Society Garden Party at BAC's Flight Test Centre at Wisley on 5 June 1966 as G-AIDN, when flown by Vivian Bellamy who took part in the Kings Cup air race – with the race number '99' on the fin. At the time of writing, this Spitfire is back in the UK after a long period in the US. (BAE SYSTEMS)

Four Spitfire Tr 9s of the Irish Air Corps. The nearest machine '162', ex-ML407, is well known on the display circuit today, flown by Carolyn Grace – still in its two-seat configuration. It currently flies in the colours it wore whilst the 'mount' of Flying Officer Johnnie Houlton DFC of 485 (New Zealand) Squadron, who was accredited, whilst flying ML407, with the first enemy aircraft shot down over the Normandy Beachhead on D-Day.

Two-seat Spitfire Tr 9 of the Irish Air Corps '161' ex-PV202 in her original light grey green finish in the early 1950s.
This Spitfire has recently been restored to flying condition by Historic Flying Ltd in the colours and configuration you see here.

Left: Spitfire F24s, the last Spitfire fighter to see operational service with the RAF, lie with their backs severed in sad rows awaiting the smelter at Wroughton in Wiltshire in the 1950s. Who would have thought in years to come the value that airframes like these would attain.

IN June 1957, after a distinguished career lasting close on 19 years, the Spitfire passed out of regular RAF service. When the Meteorological Flight received its Mosquitoes it passed three of its Spitfire XIXs to the newly-formed RAF Historic Aircraft Flight at Biggin Hill. This was the predecessor of today's Battle of Britain Memorial Flight. Its remit was to maintain these iconic aircraft in a flying condition for as long as possible, to commemorate significant national anniversaries and also to demonstrate the aircraft at air shows.

By that time the number of airworthy Spitfires around the world was falling rapidly until by the mid-1960s only 10 remained. The RAF's Historic Aircraft Flight operated two Mk XIXs. The Israeli Air Force retained a Mk IX which it flew occasionally, while the Belgian company COGEA operated four Mk IXs to tow banner targets for anti-aircraft gunners. And three Spitfires in Britain were in private hands: the British Aircraft Corporation owned a Mk V, John Fairey owned a Mk VIII converted to a two-seater, and Rolls-Royce owned a Mk XIV.

The watershed in Spitfire preservation fortunes came in 1969 with the epic film *The Battle of Britain*. For the air-to-air combat scenes the production company assembled a contingent of a dozen flyable Spitfires, about half of which it had restored to flying condition. The film was a huge box-office success and it left in its wake three important legacies that would help to secure the Spitfire's survival in the years to come. First, it boosted interest in surviving airworthy Spitfires, leading to

spontaneous applause whenever one took part in an air show. Secondly, it showed that almost anyone, provided he or she was wealthy enough, could own and perhaps even fly a Spitfire. And thirdly it showed that a team of enthusiasts, with the necessary skills and with time to spare, could restore a Spitfire 'wreck' to an airworthy condition.

Enter some larger-than-life characters, men with considerable personal wealth, who were willing to commit the large sums of money necessary to give substance to their dream of flying one of these aircraft. One was Doug Arnold, then the owner of Blackbushe airport. In 1976 he visited India with Spitfire historian Peter Arnold (no relation) to look over a number of Spitfires reported to be in a dilapidated condition at airfields around the country. Doug Arnold purchased four of the least decrepit airframes and had them shipped to Blackbushe for restoration. Other enthusiasts followed his lead and eventually 'the Indian connection' yielded no fewer than 16 Spitfire airframes, most of which have since been restored to flying condition. A similar search in Israel yielded three Spitfire IX airframes that had

The present-day works of Airframe Assemblies at Sandown, Isle of Wight. This firm turns out major replacement assemblies for reconstructed Spitfires and other aircraft types.

spent a decade or more sitting in the open at various Kibbutz playgrounds.

Another useful source of Spitfire airframes was the so-called 'gate guardian' aircraft outside RAF stations. The years had not been kind to these airframes, which had sat in the wind and the weather for decades. In the late 1980s Tim Routsis, owner of Historic Flying Limited (HFL), made an unusual offer to the Ministry of Defence in London. In return for a number of these Spitfire airframes, he offered to supply several full-size fibreglass replicas of Spitfires and Hurricanes to replace them, as well as other inducements. Coated with a durable weatherproof finish, these 'ultimate Airfix' replacements could sit outside almost indefinitely without serious deterioration. The MoD accepted the offer. Having been launched on one of these restoration projects, a team committed itself to an enormous amount of work. Several years, in some cases a decade or more, would elapse before the results of their labours could take to the skies.

From the mid-1980s to the mid-1990s a trickle of beautifully restored Spitfires returned to the air as various restoration projects bore fruit. This movement passed an important milestone on 5 May 1996 during a 'Southampton Salutes the Spitfire' fly-past to mark the 60th anniversary of the prototype's first flight when 13 airworthy Spitfires were assembled at Eastleigh Airport, scene of the fighter's maiden flight. They then took off and assembled in formation behind noted air display pilot 'Hoof' Proudfoot to fly past the Western Shore

and the sites of the old Supermarine factories at Woolston and Itchen. Police estimated that around 80,000 spectators turned out to watch – and applaud – the spectacle.

The process of restoring Spitfires has continued. During the Duxford air display on 9 and 10 September 2000 to commemorate the 60th anniversary of the Battle of Britain, 21 airworthy Spitfires flew into the airfield and 20 of them took part in the grand fly-past on each of the two days. At the time of writing more than 60 Spitfires are in an airworthy or nearly airworthy state, around the world. And work is well advanced on several more.

On this basis the success of the grand fly-past of Spitfires over Southampton in 2036 to commemorate the centenary of the first prototype's flight seems assured.

Top left: Castle Bromwich it ain't! Interior of the Airframe Assemblies hangar at Sandown, showing in the foreground jigs for the simultaneous construction of three Spitfire fuselages.

Steve Vizard, proprietor of Airframe Assemblies, inspects a replacement wing for a Spitfire.

How many airworthy Spitfires are there now, worldwide?

The author acknowledges the invaluable assistance given by Peter Arnold in the preparation of this Section. So, how many airworthy Spitfires are there now, worldwide? That is a difficult question. It all hinges on how one defines the word 'airworthy'. Does it include only those Spitfires that could be wheeled out of their hangar tomorrow morning, their engine started and then able to take off? In that case the answer is 'somewhere around 20', although the exact number will fluctuate from day-to-day. Much depends on the time of the year, for that would exclude aircraft undergoing their annual winter-scheduled maintenance and repair. It also excludes previously airworthy Spitfires undergoing rebuilds, and aircraft suffering damage but under repair for flight. Then there are aircraft that were flying until recently, but whose owners had decided to put them in a museum or in storage for 'a rest'.

Rather than ask a question that cannot be answered with accuracy, it is more productive if the question can be rephrased. The low point for the number of airworthy Spitfires was during the mid-1960s when only ten such machines existed in the world. Then in 1969 came the film *The Battle of Britain*, which sparked off interest in restoring Spitfires to flying condition.

This author believes that the best indicator of the number of Spitfires now flyable, or potentially flyable, is to list those flown or restored to flight since 1969. At the time of writing, December 2009, that number stands at 73 Spitfires and Seafires. Of the 73 listed in the schedule below, 47 are fully airworthy provided time spent on the ground for routine maintenance is disregarded.

No.	RAF	Civil Reg.	Mk. No.	Owner/Custodian	Location	Status
1	AR213	G-AIST	F. Mk. Ia	Sheringham Aviation	Duxford UK	Fully airworthy
2	P7350	Military	F. Mk. IIa	MoD	Coningsby, UK	Fully airworthy
3	AB910	Military	LF. Mk.Vb	MoD	Coningsby, UK	Fully airworthy
4	AR501	G-AWII	LF. Mk.Vc	Shuttleworth Trust	Old Warden, UK	Under major refurbishment
5	AR614	N614VC	F. Mk.Vc	Paul Allen / FHC	Seattle, Washington USA	Fully airworthy
6	BL628	N628BL	F. Mk.Vb	Rod Lewis	Texas, USA	Fully airworthy
7	BM597	G-MKVB	F. Mk.Vb	Guy Black / HAC	Duxford, UK	Fully airworthy
8	EE606	G-MKVC	F. Mk.Vc	David Arnold	(Parts only)	Total write-off. Crash
9	EP120	G-LFVB	F. Mk.Vb	Stephen Grey / TFC	Duxford, UK	Fully airworthy
10	JG891	N624TB	F. Mk.Vc (trop)	Tom Friedkin	Texas, USA	Fully airworthy
11	MT719	N719MT	LF. Mk.VIII	Jim Cavanaugh / CFM	Dallas, Texas, USA	Fully airworthy
12	MT818	G-AIDN	TR. Mk.VIII	Paul Andrews	Kemble, UK	Under major refurbishment
13	MV154	G-BKMI	HF. Mk.VIII	Rob Lamplough	Filton, UK	Fully airworthy
14	MV239	VH-HET	HF. Mk.VIII	David Lowy	Temora, Australia	Fully airworthy
15	NH631	Military	LF. Mk.VIII	Indian A/F Hist. Flight	Palam, India	Flying suspended
16	MA793	N930LB	F. Mk. IX	TAM Museum	Sao Carlos, Brazil	Museum display
17	MH367	ZK-WDQ	TR, Mk IX	Tom Brooking	Ardmore, New Zealand	Damaged in landing accident. Undergoing repair
18	MH434	G-ASJV	LF. Mk. IX	Old Flying Machine Co	Duxford, UK	Fully airworthy
19	MH415	N415MH	LF. Mk. IX	Wilson Edwards	Big Spring, Texas, USA	Long term storage
20	MJ627	G-BMSB	TR. Mk. IX	Maurice Bayliss	'An RAF Station', UK	Fully airworthy
21	MJ730	N730MJ	LF. Mk. IX	Jerry Yagen	Suffolk, Virginia, USA	Fully airworthy
22	MJ772	N8R	TR. Mk. IX	Doug Champlin	Seattle, Washington USA	Museum display
23	MK297	NXBL	LF. Mk. IX	*	Hamilton, Canada	Total write-off. Fire
24	MK356	Military	LF. Mk. IX	MoD	Coningsby, UK	Fully airworthy
25	MK732	PH-OUQ	LF. Mk. IX	RNethAF Hist Flight	Gilze Rijen, Netherlands	Fully airworthy/accident repair
26	MK912	C-FFLC	LF. Mk. IX	Ed Russell	Niagara, Canada	Fully airworthy
27	MK923	N521R	LF. Mk. IX	Craig McCaw / MoF	Seattle, Washington, USA	Museum display
28	MK959	N959RT	LF. Mk. IX	Tom Duffy	Milville, New Jersey, USA	Fully airworthy

29	ML407	G-LFIX	TR. Mk. IX	Carolyn Grace	Bentwaters/Duxford, UK	Fully airworthy
30	ML417	N2F	LF. Mk. IX	Tom Freidkin	Texas, USA	Fully airworthy
31	NH238	G-MKIX	LF. Mk. IXe	David Arnold	Greenham Common	Long-term storage
32	PL344	G-IXCC	F. Mk. IX	Tom Blair	Duxford, UK	Fully airworthy
33	PT462	G-CTIX	TR. Mk. IX	Anthony Hodgson	Bryn Gwyn Bach, UK	Fully airworthy
34	PV202	G-CCCA	TR. Mk. IX	Karel Bos / HFL	Duxford, UK	Fully airworthy
35	PV270	ZK-SPI	Mk.IX	Brendon Deere	Ohakea, NZ	Fully airworthy
36	SM520	G-GILDA	Tr.Mk. IX	Steve Brooks	Filton, UK	Fully airworthy
37	TA805	G-PMNF	HF. MK. IX	Peter Monk	Biggin Hill, UK	Fully airworthy
38	TE213	Military	HF. Mk. IXe	SAAF Museum Flight	Lanseria, South Africa	Major accident - Stored
39	TE308	N308WK	TR. Mk. IX	Bill Greenwood	Aspen, Colorado, USA	Fully airworthy/accident repair
40	TE554	Military	LF. Mk. IXe	Israeli Air Force Musem	Beersheba, Israel	Fully airworthy
41	TE566	VH-IXT	LF. Mk. IXe	Aviation Australia	Brisbane, Australia	Major accident - Stored
42	PL965	G-MKXI	PR. Mk. XI	Peter Teichman	North Weald, UK	Fully airworthy
43	PL983	G-PRXI	PR. Mk. XI	Propshop / HFL	Duxford, UK	Under major refurbishment
44	MV293	G-BGHB	FR. Mk. XIVe	Stephen Grey / TFC	Duxford, UK	Fully airworthy
45	NH749	NX749DP	FR. Mk. XIVe	Commemorative Air Force	Camarillo, California, USA	Under major refurbishment
46	NH799	ZK-XIV	FR. Mk. XIV	Murray Miers	Ardmore, New Zealand	Under major refurbishment
47	NH904	N114BP	FR. Mk. XIV	Bob Pond	Palm Springs, Ca, USA	Fully airworthy
48	RM689	G-ALGT	F. Mk. XIVe	Rolls Royce	Bristol, UK	Under major refurbishment
49	RN201	G-BSKP	F. Mk. XIVe	Tom Blair / Spitfire Ltd	Kissimmee, Florida,USA	Fully airworthy
50	SM832	N54SF	F. Mk. XIVe	Tom Freidkin	Chino, California, USA	Fully airworthy
51	TZ138	C-GSPT	FR. Mk. XIVe	Robert Jens	Vancouver, Canada	Airworthy, resting
52	RR263	Military	LF. Mk. XVIe	Musee de l'Air	Paris, France	Museum display
53	RW382	NX382RW	LF. Mk. XVIe	Pemberton Billing	I.O.W. UK	Under major refurbishment
54	RW386	G-BXVI	LF. Mk. XVIe	Biltima Sweden Holdings AB	Engelholm, Sweden	Fully airworthy
55	SL721	C-GVZB	LF. Mk. XVIe	Michael Potter	Ottawa, Canada	Fully airworthy
56	TB863	VH-XVI	LF. Mk. XVIe	David Lowy	Temora, Australia	Fully airworthy
57	TD248	G-OXVI	LF. Mk. XVIe	Tom Blair / Spitfire Ltd	Duxford, UK	Fully airworthy
58	TE184	G-MXVI	LF. Mk. XVIe	Paul Andrews	Booker UK	Fully airworthy
59	TE356	N356EV	LF. Mk. XVIe	Evergreen Ventures	McMinnville, Oregon, USA	Museum display
60	TE384	N384TE	LF. Mk. XVIe	Ken McBride	Hollister, Ca, USA	Long-term storage
61	TE392	N97RW	LF. Mk. XVIe	Robert Waltrip / LSFM	Galveston, Texas, USA	Fully airworthy/Flood damaged
62	TE476	N476TE	LF. Mk. XVIe	Kermit Weeks	Polk City, Florida, USA	Museum display
63	SM845	G-BUOS	FR. Mk. XVIIIe	Biltima Sweden Holdings AB	Engelholm, Sweden	Fully airworthy
64	SM969	N969SM	F. Mk. XVIIIe	Jim Beasley	Coatesville, Philadelphia, USA	Fully airworthy
65	TP280	N280TP	FR. Mk. XVIIIe	Rudy Frasca	Urbana, Illinois, USA	Fully airworthy
66	TP298	N41702	FR. Mk. XVIIIe	Murray Gilchrist	I.O.W. UK	Major accident - Stored
67	PM631	Military	PR. Mk. XIX	MoD	Coningsby, UK	Fully airworthy
68	PS853	G-RRGN	PR. Mk. XIX	Rolls Royce	Filton/East Midlands, UK	Fully airworthy
69	PS890	F-AZJS	PR. Mk. XIX	Cristophe Jacquard	Dijon, France	Fully airworthy
70	PS915	Military	PR. Mk. XIX	MoD	Coningsby, UK	Fully airworthy
71	PK350	Military	F. Mk. 22	*	Harare, Zimbabwe	Total write-off. Crash
72	SX336	G-KASX	F. MkXVII Sea.	Tim Manna	North Weald, UK	Fully airworthy
73	VP441	N47SF	FR. Mk47 Sea	Jim Smith	Crystal Lakes, Montana, USA	Fully airworthy

23 Fully airworthy in UK
47 Fully airworthy World-Wide

Spitfire Mk Vb, BM597 struts its stuff at an air display bearing the JH code letters of No 317 (Polish) Squadron. (Philip Makanna 'GHOSTS'),

Interesting hybrid: Mark XIX serial PS890 was powered by a Griffon 57 engine with a contra-rotating airscrew, taken from a retired Shackleton maritime patrol aircraft. More recently that engine was replaced with a regular Griffon and 5-bladed propeller. The aircraft belongs to Cristoph Jaquard and is registered in France.

Seen at Duxford in 2008 was another of the newest Spitfires to join the club of restored aircraft, Mk XVIII serial SM969 in the post-war markings of No 28 Squadron.

Left: Battle Of Britain Memorial Flight Supermarine Spitfire Mk LF IXe, MK356.

This Spitfire Mk XIVe, RM689, is owned by Rolls Royce, and is currently under major refurbishment.
The aircraft wears the MN code letters of No 350 (Belgian) Squadron, with which it saw action early in 1945.

A Spitfire PR. XIX of the Battle of Britain Memorial Flight.

'Spitfire Row' at the Battle of Britain Memorial Flight hangar at Coningsby with the aircraft dismantled and undergoing full inspections after the end of the air display season. At the time of writing the Flight's Spitfire complement comprises a Mk II, a Mk V, a Mk IX and two Mk XIXs.

Appendix I

THE SPITFIRE FAMILY

Mk I first production fighter version, powered by the Rolls-Royce Merlin III engine; made its maiden flight in May 1938 and entered service in September.

Mk PR I reconnaissance aircraft designated from IA to IG, depending on the configuration of the cameras and the additional internal fuel tankage. **PR IA** was a modified Mk I fighter with the armament removed and a 5 in focal length camera mounted vertically in each wing; two aircraft were delivered and began operations in November 1939. **PR IB** was similar to PR IA but with additional 29-gal fuel tank behind cockpit. **PR IC** was similar to the PR 1B but with 30-gal blister tank under the port wing and two vertically mounted cameras in a blister under the starboard wing. **PR ID** was a much-modified Mk I with 61-gal integral tank in the leading edge of each wing and a 29-gal tank in the rear fuselage; two vertically-mounted cameras were behind the cockpit and this was the most numerous Spitfire PR variant of the early war years, later re-designated **PR Mk IV**. **PR IE** was an unarmed variant optimised for low-altitude oblique photography with a bulge under each wing to accommodate a camera pointing outwards and a small angle downwards; only one, N3117, modified. **PR IF** was also unarmed with a 30-gal fuel tank under each wing and one 29-gal fuel tank and two vertically-mounted cameras in the fuselage. **PR IG** was armed and optimised for low-level oblique photography; it retained the eight .303 inch guns for self defence; one 29-gal fuel tank and one oblique and two vertical cameras behind the cockpit.

Mk II fighter variant similar to Mk I but fitted with Merlin XII engine; entered service in September 1940.

Mk V fighter version developed from Mk I but with Merlin 45 Series engine; entered service in February 1941 and built in very large numbers; during mid-war period was the first variant fitted with bomb racks to allow it to operate in fighter-bomber role.

Mk VI high-altitude interceptor developed from Mk V but fitted with pressurised cabin and longer span wing; powered by Merlin 47 engine which included an additional blower for cabin pressurisation; built in small numbers and entered service in April 1942.

Mk VII high-altitude interceptor developed from Mk VI but powered by two-stage supercharged Merlin 61 Series and built in moderate numbers; first squadron became operational in April 1943.

Mk VIII general-purpose fighter developed from Mk VII but without pressurised cabin; entered service in summer 1943 and although built in large numbers, all served outside UK; also saw widespread use as fighter-bomber.

Mk IX general purpose fighter developed from Mk V but fitted with Merlin 61 Series engine; entered service in June 1942 and although intended as stop-gap pending large-scale production of Mk VIII, remained in production until the end of the war, built in greater numbers than any other variant; also operated in fighter-bomber and fighter-reconnaissance roles; late production aircraft fitted with cut-back rear fuselages and bubble canopies.

Mk X photographic reconnaissance variant with PR1D's enlarged internal fuel tankage but fitted with the Merlin 61 Series engine and pressurised cabin; entered service in May 1944 and built in small numbers.

Mk XI photographic reconnaissance variant similar to Mk X but without pressurised cabin; despite the later mark number, it entered service in December 1942, some time ahead of Mk X; became the most-used photographic reconnaissance variant of mid-war period.

Mk XII fighter version developed from Mk V but fitted with single-stage supercharged Griffon II engine; built in moderate numbers as a low-altitude fighter, production aircraft having clipped wings; entered service February 1943.

Mk XIII fighter reconnaissance version with vertical and oblique cameras and four .303 inch machine guns; entered service and only a few built.

Mk XIV fighter version developed from Mk VIII but with two-stage supercharged Griffon 61 Series engine; entered service February 1944; final production aircraft had cut-back rear fuselage and bubble canopy; fighter-reconnaissance version went into service in small numbers with vertical and oblique cameras in rear fuselage.

Mk XVI general purpose fighter similar to Mk IX but powered by Merlin 266 engine produced under licence in the USA by Packard; entered service in September 1944, late production aircraft being fitted with cut-back rear fuselage and bubble canopy; also operated as fighter-bomber.

Mk XVIII fighter-bomber version developed from Mk XIV powered by Griffon 61 Series engine and bubble canopy; also featured redesigned and strengthened wing and additional fuel tanks in the rear fuselage; entered service 1945 too late for wartime action; fighter-reconnaissance version also appeared.

Mk XIX definitive photographic reconnaissance variant combining Griffon 61 series engine and pressurised cabin and with Mk XI's wing leading edge tanks; entered service in the summer of 1944 and became the most-used reconnaissance variant during war's final year.

Mk 21 fighter version with redesigned and strengthened wing and fuselage, powered by Griffon 61 Series engine; entered service in April 1945 and saw some action before the war ended; was first variant to be designated by Arabic numbers instead of Roman numerals.

Mk 22 fighter version similar to Mk 21 but with cut-back rear fuselage and bubble canopy; production aircraft fitted with an enlarged tailplane, fin and rudder; entered service in November 1947 and became main post-war production variant, remaining in service with Royal Auxiliary Air Force squadrons until 1951.

Mk 24 fighter version based on Mk 22 but fitted with two additional fuel tanks in the rear fuselage and wing fittings to carry six 60 lb rockets; only one squadron operated this variant which remained in front-line RAF service until January 1952.

Appendix 2

DEVELOPMENT OF THE SPITFIRE

From the time of its maiden flight the Spitfire underwent continual series of incremental improvements to improve its performance. By squeezing progressively more power out of the Merlin, and later the Griffon, series of engines, Rolls-Royce provided the impetus for many of these changes.

As it is rarely possible to get something for nothing there was a downside to almost every step in the development process. With each increase in engine power there was a rise in engine weight and a corresponding increase in fuel consumption. To restore the aircraft's range it required larger capacity and therefore heavier fuel tanks. To convert that additional engine power into thrust without increasing airscrew diameter, the Spitfire's propeller acquired additional blades. It progressed from a two-bladed unit on early production aircraft to a three-bladed one, a four-bladed one and finally to a five-bladed propeller. The greater the number of blades on a propeller, the greater its weight and also the greater the twisting force it exerted on the airframe. To balance out these forces, there needed to be increases in the area of the tail surfaces. On production Spitfire Mks 22 and 24 the tail surfaces underwent a complete redesign and became much larger.

The lessons learned in air combat imposed other increases in weight as various new items of equipment were added such as armour protection for the pilot and vulnerable parts of the structure. Also, as the war progressed, the Spitfire needed more powerful and therefore heavier armament. In straight and level flight an aircraft could cope relatively easily with progressive increases in weight. But air-to-air combat was another matter. When the pilot needed to throw his fighter around and pull 6G in a tight turn every part of the structure weighed six times as much. If it had not been stressed to withstand the additional forces, the airframe might simply collapse. To cope with each major increase in weight, therefore, the internal structure had to be strengthened to restore the safe load factors. And, as night followed day, each bout of strengthening brought with it a further increase in weight.

In the history of aviation no other aircraft design was so continuously, so aggressively, so thoroughly and so successfully developed as the Spitfire. The various changes produced a huge increase in its fighting ability. As a result the Spitfire retained its place in the forefront of fighter design from the biplane era until the early years of the jet age. In the course of that development the Spitfire's engine power almost doubled, from the 1,030 hp of the Merlin II engine of the Spitfire I, to the 2,035 hp of the Griffon 61 engine fitted to Spitfire 21. Maximum speed increased by just over a quarter, from the 362 mph of the Mk I to the 457 mph attained by the Mk 21. The maximum rate of climb more than doubled, from the 2,195 feet per minute of the Mark I to 4,900 feet per minute of the Mk 21. Firepower was increased by a factor of five. A 3-second burst from the eight rifle-calibre machine guns of the Mk I loosed off rounds weighing 8 lbs, while a similar burst from the Spitfire 21's four 20 mm cannon loosed off projectiles weighing 40 lbs. At the same time, the normal maximum take-off weight rose by more than two-thirds, from 5,280 lbs for the Mk I to 9,124 lbs for the Mk 21.

Appendix 3

BASIC SPECIFICATIONS OF MAIN PRODUCTION SPITFIRE FIGHTER VARIANTS

	Mk I	Mk V	Mk XI	Mk XII	Mk XIV	Mk 21
Span	36ft 10in	36ft 10in	36ft 10in	36ft 10in	36ft 10in	40ft 4in
Length	29ft 11in	29ft 11in	30ft 0in	30ft 9in	32ft 8in	32ft 8in
Max take-off weight	5819lb	6525lb	7400lb	7415lb	8400lb	9124lb
Power	Merlin II, 1,030hp	Merlin 45, 1,470hp	Merlin 61, 1,560hp	Griffon IIB, 1,700hp	Griffon 61, 2,035hp	Griffon 61, 2,035hp
Max speed	362mph	371mph	409mph	397mph	446mph	457mph
Service ceiling	31,900ft	37,500ft	38,000ft	32,800ft	44,000ft	43,000ft
Gun armament	8x.303in	2x20mm, 4x.303in	2x20mm, 4x.303in	2x20mm, 4x.303in	2x20mm, 4x.303in	4x20mm

Notes: Mk I information relates to the first production Spitfire, K9787, during its service trials in May 1938; Mk V, to an early production aircraft, W3134, during its trials in May 1941; Mk IX, to the converted Mark V, AB505, during its trials in April 1942; Mk XII, to the prototype, DP845, during its trials in September 1942 when it had full span wings; production Mark XIIs had clipped wings; Mk XIV, to JF319, a converted Mk VIII, during its trials in September 1943 and Mk 21, to the prototype, PP139, during trials in 1943 when it was fitted with extended-span wings; production Mark 21s had rounded wing tips, span 36ft 11in.